Chalk Dust Dreams

Chalk Dust Dreams

by
Cleo Winslett Schiewitz Leissner, *1898 –*

The Naylor Company
Book Publishers of the Southwest
San Antonio, Texas

Library of Congress Cataloging in Publication Data

Leissner, Cleo Winslett Schiewitz, 1898-
    Chalk dust dreams.

    1. Leissner, Cleo Winslett Schiewitz, 1898-
I. Title
LA2317.L56A33   371.1'0092'4 [B]   74-7492
ISBN 0-8111-0531-8

43,897

DEDICATION

To the Past, the Present, and the Future:

To the memory of Mama, Papa, and Gus, whose love for me and belief in me gave me faith "to move mountains"

To Floyd, my son, and Brodie, his wife, and to my Jake, who daily bring me contentment, happiness, and pride

To Carolyn and Pat, my precious grandchildren, with whom my dreams are now entrusted

CONTENTS

PART ONE: If a Task Is Once Begun
1. I Dream a Dream   3
2. See a Vision   4
3. Find an Enemy (Cotton)   7
4. Spell to Read   9
5. Acquire a Friend   14
6. Meet a Master Teacher   15
7. Become a Celebrity   22
8. Am Almost Sidetracked   27
9. Earn a High School Diploma   29
10. And Achieve My Holy Grail   30

PART TWO: Never Leave It Till It's Done
1. I Glimpse Paradise   37
2. Go for a Buggy Ride   40
3. Live Through a Day in Purgatory   45
4. Make New Friends   47
5. Bless a Black Cat   49
6. Work and Play   51
7. Win the Battle of the Buggy Whip   56
8. Commit a Faux Pas   62
9. Suffer Public Embarrassment   63
10. And Make a Difficult Decision   66

PART THREE: Be the Labor Great or Small
1. I Discover a Nightmare   71

2.	Learn Its Cause	75
3.	Win the First Skirmish	77
4.	Live Through Another First Day	79
5.	Battle Ignorance and Intolerance	81
6.	Bring "Sandy Claws" to Lost Creek	84
7.	Find a Generous, Gentle Heart	87
8.	Earn a Strange Loyalty	91
9.	Enjoy a Formal Visit	93
10.	Build a Program	94
11.	Know the Play Must Go On	97
12.	And Make My Greatest Decision	102

PART FOUR: Do It Well or Not at All

1.	I Live and Laugh and Grieve	109
2.	Answer the Chalk Dust Call	113
3.	Establish a Little Republic	114
4.	And Would Buy That Dream Again	118

PART ONE

If a Task Is Once Begun

1

I'm going to be a schoolteacher!
I'm going to teach school when I get big!
I'm going to read stories!
I'm going to spell everybody down!

Thus chanted a grimy little four-year-old girl as she skipped along the bare, dusty lane that led away from Bug Scuffle School.

I — this grimy, excited little girl was I — had spent the day, which was Friday, in school while Mama and Papa had gone to town to see a doctor about Papa's increasing illness. With two older brothers and two older sisters to carry me when I grew tired on the more-than-three-miles-to-school hike, I experienced little weariness, for my day at school — the first in my life — had opened a new, wonderful world to me. I had drawn pictures on the board, played with the boys and girls at recess, listened to enchanting snatches of stories; and finally, curling up in the lap of the beautiful, sweet-smelling young teacher, I had gone blissfully to sleep while my beautiful lady gave out spelling words to a group who stood in a long line against the wall. As I drifted off to sleep, I wished I could stand in a line like that and spell magic words. I had no inkling then of the dread in the hearts of those spellers as they waited for the fateful word whose misspelling meant they would be passed by a luckier or better speller, and so become the object of pity or ridicule, both devastating to a child's pride. To me, as I lay relaxed in the lap of my new idol, school meant enchantment, mystery, magic.

When I told the teacher good-bye, I whispered shyly, "I'm going to be a teacher just like you." My brother, who stood by impatiently waiting for me (he was already waiting for the day Papa would let him quit school) gave a loud guffaw, snatched me up, and marched down the lane with me toward home. But neither the jibes of my brothers nor the gentler ridicule of my sisters could kill the dream born in Bug Scuffle School that winter day.

2

It was in this same unpainted, one-room country school that I had another experience which increased my longing for something better than a poor sandy-land farm and ranch, lost in a forest of brush and cactus. Shortly after school started in the fall after I had made up my mind to be a teacher, my sisters and brothers ran home with the news that on the next night an unbelievable program was to be presented at school. A man was bringing a talking machine; and for a small admission, people in the community could hear this wonder of the age. Though my now-very-sick dad assured us that he had a house full of talking machines and that hearing another would be no novelty, we were among the first at school the next night.

When the magic horn, a giant morning glory, was turned directly toward my brother and me, seated on the recitation bench so we would miss nothing, and "Uncle Josh" began one of his famous humorous harangues, I was sure someone was talking under the mysteriously draped table on which the "phonygraph" (as the exhibitor called it) rested. Determined to expose the fraud, I crawled under the table to find the talker, greatly amusing the few worldly-wise who were present, and just as greatly embarrassing my family. My mother hauled me to the back of the room just as I was about to poke my head into the big horn to look for the speaker. For years after this, if I showed undue curiosity — a frequent tendency of mine — some member of the family would remark, "She's looking for the man in the phonygraph."

But I was, that night, fired with a new ambition — we must own a talking machine, not to hear Uncle Josh, but to thrill to the glorious music that came from that morning-glory horn. The only music in my life prior to this had been the sound of a wheezy pump organ at church, the sound of my dad's lovely baritone Irish voice as he rocked and sang to me after supper, or the wail of my brother's French harp as he played it and taught me to dance in the backyard — an activity taboo in our community, where dancing was considered one of the Devil's most potent weapons.

Two or three years later, when I saw my first movie, a crude Western projected on a sheet hung over a blackboard in another country school, I again was completely enthralled with this strange new phenomenon; and again I embarrassed my family by dashing to the back of the room to keep the big, white, galloping horse from running right over me as he dashed out on the makeshift screen. Again I was consumed with a desire to know how such strange things could be. Others knew, and I must know too.

In a spite of a dogged determination that I would make no more such blunders, I again made a fool of myself — this time at church and before the scandalized eyes of the entire body of churchgoers. An old-fashioned revival meeting was in progress in the little church we so faithfully attended. The sermon was long and highly emotional. The evangelist insisted again and again in thundering tones that his brand of religion would open a new world to us, one in which we could dream great dreams and see great visions. I was not particularly interested in dreams or visions just then. The picnic lunch that was to follow the sermon offered greater charms to me, for I had been glued to that hard bench, growing increasingly hungry for hours, it seemed. I longed for food and freedom. Consequently, I was among the first to reach the front door when the exhortation finally came to an end, though for evident reasons I had been sitting very near the front with my mother.

Just as I sailed down the front steps, I heard a strange noise indeed. Looking up the hill toward the sound, I knew instantly that I really "had religion," for I was looking at a startling vision!

Down that hill came a bright red, buggy-like contraption pulled by no horses but apparently propelled by a man wearing an enveloping wrap that flew in the wind like a Mother Hubbard. On his head was a baseball cap with an over-sized crown, and protecting his eyes was a modified version of a baseball catcher's mask. With his gloved hands, he grasped a small wheel instead of the usual buggy line; and, sitting like a conquering hero, he looked neither to right nor left.

As the red vehicle swept by at a terrific rate of speed (all of fifteen miles per hour) and horses reared at their hitching posts, I realized that my vision was vanishing. With a desperate shout, "Wait for me!" I dashed from the church grounds and down the road over which the red vision was chugging in a cloud of churning dust. I almost caught it before I gave out completely, but I really "caught it" when my mother finally got me home.

That was one dinner-on-the-ground our family missed, for taking their stupid little girl and their well-filled picnic basket, they drove the eight miles back home in disgrace. Only the marvel of the red horseless buggy, I am sure, prevented my untimely death from hunger and dread of what awaited me at home. Now I had a fourth consuming desire: I must ride in an automobile, and I must know what made it run.

3

We had some disastrous years, losing all our crops in a hurricane and a flood, and nearly all our range cattle and other livestock from some strange disease. Papa's illness had developed into a serious case of inflammatory rheumatism, which made him an invalid for three years. For more than one year he was confined to his bed, another to crutches; and later he walked with the aid of a cane. Every child big enough to drag a cotton sack or swing a hoe had to work in the fields to help support the family — no easy task with cotton at five cents a pound, or even less, and a big family to support, plus heavy doctor bills to pay.

At first Papa had insisted I was too little to work in the fields; so I spent many hours sitting by his bed, "reading" to him from textbooks owned by the older children — we had no other books except the huge family Bible. I would choose a picture in a book and then "read" the story to him. He always insisted that my stories were much more interesting than those really in the book. Even when I had to lend my energies to such irksome tasks as rocking my new little sister in her cradle or pulling and pushing a dasher up and down in a churn, I was creating stories to tell my dad so that I could bring a smile to his pain-tortured face.

Things were particularly bad the summer I was seven,

and for a time it seemed that we would not be able to start to school when it opened the first week in October, for we must first harvest the crop. We had now left our small farm and ranch in Karnes County — the home of my father's people for generations — and were renting a farm up in the hills in Gonzales County near Hochheim. All summer, as I dragged a heavy cotton sack and pulled the stubborn King Cotton from his torturous bolls, I lived in a frenzy of anticipation. This was the time I had been living for. At last I was going to school. At last I could learn to be a teacher!

When our ability to finish gathering the extremely late and unusually bountiful crops in time to start to school seemed doubtful, life became a daily torture. I drove myself and begged the others to work harder and longer each day. How I loathed the sight of the rows of white stalks stretching on and on, standing between me and my dream of school. My mild dislike for cotton turned into bitter hatred.

One torrid, unbearable day near the end of September, when it seemed we had hardly made a dent in the harvest, and the opening of school was less than a week away, I was overcome with despair. Throwing myself on my half-filled cotton sack, I was dissolved in tears when Papa hobbled up, painfully sat down beside me, and gathered me into his gentle arms. The look of suffering on his face that day has remained with me always. Not even when his illness was most acute had he worn such an expression of torture.

"Take your sack to the wagon, Daughter, and go on to the house. You need a day off," he comforted. "You're such a little thing and so tired."

"I'm not tired," I wailed. "I've got to go to school next week. I've just got to go. How can I be a teacher when I can't even read? I hate cotton, but I can't go to school, and I'll have to spend the rest of my life bent over a cotton stalk!"

8

☆　☆　☆

In a family conference held that night, around the long dining table flanked by backless, hard benches on each side and lighted by two flickering kerosene lamps, it was decided that I might start to school on Monday, while the older children, who had never liked school much anyway, would continue the field work. To pay for this privilege, I must hurry home each day, bring in wood, shuck corn for the stock, and help Mama with supper. Then after supper I was to help clean up the dishes. Never did the prospect of such hard tasks seem so pleasant. Before the end of the year I, a seven-year-old girl, was preparing the evening meal for a family of eight, though I had to stand on a box to reach the mixing bowl. And I loved it!

4

On Monday morning my oldest brother, who at the age of sixteen had assumed the responsibilities of a man because of my father's illness, walked with me over the rocky hills to the little unpainted shack almost hidden in weeds. Though it was four miles from home, it was the shortest four miles I had ever walked — and the longest.

We had hardly reached the school yard when a vision of loveliness (or so she then seemed to me) appeared at the door and clanged a raucous call from a large bell in her hand. From every direction came stiffly starched, beribboned girls and freshly-scrubbed, spick-and-span boys.

This new community into which we had moved was made up almost entirely of homeowners with comfortable incomes, and their children felt superior to the children of any family classified as tenant farmers. My entry, therefore, merited little notice from either the teacher or the pupils. I sat on the front seat, a habit of mine that no unpleasant experiences had altered; and the fact that I sat alone disturbed me not at all. I was still in an enchanted world.

Before many days had passed, I knew my teacher was totally unlike my idol back at Bug Scuffle. She was a snob, though, of course, I did not know the word for her then. Caring more for a fashion-plate pupil than for one eager to learn, she catered to the children of prominent families in the community, at the expense of those from poorer homes. We were divided into two groups — the Desirables and the Undesirables — and I, as the daughter of a tenant farmer, was promptly relegated to the latter group. I had not been in school many days before I developed the first of my series of precepts that have been my chief guides in my thirty-eight years of teaching.

"I wil be gud to al my pupls whether they have fine clos are not," I laboriously printed in my carefully-guarded, secret *How to Teach School* composition book. I owe the choice spelling to a very homely little boy, older than I and more advanced in knowledge, who had already learned how to spell.

But even my disillusionment with my "vision of loveliness" did not dim my interest in learning to read nor my ambition to teach school. When in a few weeks she was chased away from school by a baseball bat in the hands of one of her very favorite Desirables — the only son of the most influential trustee — and a new teacher came to replace her, conditions improved for us Undesirables. The new teacher was woefully lacking both in teaching techniques and in learning, but she was warm and human and understanding. She liked all of us, genuinely liked us. I therefore

10

added my second precept: "I will love all my pupils — even if they are poor or bad or dirty or ugly."

"C-a-t — *cat,*" I was forced to spell before I was permitted to pronounce the word, in spite of the fact that I knew it at sight.

"I — *I,* s-e-e — *see,* a — *a,* b-o-y — *boy,*" I was trained to read.

And when I asked my first teacher why I should do this when I knew the words without spelling them, she answered "Because I tell you to, and that's enough." Then she lifted the long, peeled stick which she used as a combination pointer and instrument of torture and started toward me.

Something of the outrage I felt must have stopped her. My family had already learned that I responded readily to reasoning, but that any threat of corporal punishment infuriated me beyond restraint. It was well for me that Dick finally resorted to the baseball bat, for from that day, I might just as well have been at home, for all the help I got from her.

Out of this experience grew my third precept: "Try to know why you require certain work and be ready to explain why to your pupils, and never strike or threaten a child if you can possibly help it." Naturally, it was not exactly so worded in the old composition book, but that was its meaning.

Even after the second teacher took over, I was forced to spell out each word in reading before I pronounced it. "Because," she explained, "that's just the way you learn to read and to spell too!" This method really did teach me to spell, but its ill effect on my reading rate has never been entirely overcome.

11

In the first year of school, short periods of recitation were followed by long periods of inactivity. Encouraged by my innate curiosity, I soon learned to devote this time to listening to the older children recite, as they sat just in front of me on the recitation bench or struggled over arithmetic problems at the board.

Often I monopolized the talk at the supper table with my version of the things I had heard at school — things about history, geography, physiology, and the wonderful, wonderful stories in the higher grade readers. My sisters and brothers, who had finished the fieldwork and started to school in November, tried to hold me to the bare facts; but I loftily assured them that I was getting ready to teach school, so I KNEW! How they kept from utterly exterminating me, I still wonder. My assertion usually clinched the discussion, however, for the idea of a teacher from our at-that-time poverty-stricken family was hilariously absurd. Hence my reply to their attempts to repress my imagination reduced them to uproarious laughter. I now realize that we then had no luxuries and few necessities of life; but we had laughter and love and harmony.

The fact that I could not become anything I was willing to work for apparently never entered Mama's mind, for her father had been a teacher of Latin, Greek, and theology in a boys' school in Missouri; but he had also been a narrow-minded, old-fashioned, "hellfire-and-damnation" preacher, who had refused to let his only daughter go to school. "A woman's place is in the home. Schooling makes fools of them," he contended, in answer to his wife's and daughter's supplications. All the longing Mama had once had for an education, therefore, was now bent toward my realizing my dream. And Papa — a happy-go-lucky Irishman even when ill — encouraged me to believe that I could do whatever I wanted to do. It was he who suggested that

I keep my *How to Teach School* book, and record in it all the things I wanted to remember to do and all the things I wanted to avoid when I became a teacher.

"Let's have your little *How To* book as our secret," he suggested, and I eagerly agreed. That crude, often amusing book, compiled by an ignorant little girl with an overdose of egotism, ambition, and self-confidence, did more to help me avoid the pitfalls in teaching than did any formal book on education I have ever encountered. It contained a study of the good and the bad methods practiced by all the teachers I had from my first year through high school.

When spring came, with corn and cotton to chop, no suggestion was made that I stop school to work. I had already "been through the first reader" and was well into the second; I was already able to solve many of the problems that bedeviled older pupils; and I had established a leadership of a sort on the playground, for I could outrun any other girl or boy in school, could play first base in baseball with marked skill for one so young, could bat the ball almost as well as any boy on the team, and could steal bases with the toughest of the group. When sides were chosen for Prisoner's Base or Red Rover, the first chooser (the choosers were always the two biggest boys in school) invariably chose me; and I was now among the first ones chosen when we had spelling matches. I often carried a spelling book open on my way to and from school, studying the words as I stumbled along. I was determined to become one of the Desirables, in spite of my simple clothes and my label as the daughter of a tenant farmer.

All this may sound insignificant to those who have never known the heartache a child can suffer from belonging to the underprivileged group, but that experience gave me a sympathy for and an understanding of that type of children that have remained with me all these years. My determination to help such children has been one of the strongest urges in my long teaching career.

5

My achievements at school had evidently reached the ears of the wife of the man from whom we rented our farm, for she took me under her wing as soon as school was out. She gave me a slight acquaintance with another of my consuming interests — one resulting from my "phony-graph" experience — for she owned a small Edison machine, which she encouraged me to enjoy. Better still, she owned an organ and knew how to play it. When she saw my heart in my eyes as I listened, she offered to teach me as much as she could.

As often as I was granted the time, I ran the mile that lay between our home and that of the Mayfields, and began my practice session, or lesson, under her supervision. As she had four sons and no daughters, I soon took the place in the family that a daughter would have loved. I rapidly learned to read simple notes and soon became somewhat adept at running the scales; but unfortunately as soon as I heard the melody, I ignored the notes and played by ear. Of course, I never really learned to play, but within a year I was pounding out the hymns at Church or Sunday School when Mrs. Mayfield, the organist, was absent or, according to her explanation did not feel like playing. I realize now how ignorant I really was, but at that time I thought I was a talented musician.

Mrs. Mayfield taught me another art, too, one that was not really approved by my preacher's-daughter-mother. Educated in a girls' finishing school in Virginia, Mrs. Mayfield had been trained to dance beautifully. She wanted her boys to learn, but they had little opportunity in a

14

community where dancing was rarely practiced. Often, therefore, after supper when I was spending the night there, she would teach her boys and me to dance to the music of the phonograph or her husband's fiddle.

How I loved to dance! It released all the frustrated longing for expression within me as I seemed to float above poverty or illness or the memory of my enemy — Cotton. If I had not already "dedicated my life" to teaching school, I am sure I would then have dedicated it to teaching dancing.

(One summer not many years later, when I was attending college with almost no cash, my skill in dancing came to the rescue and furnished me the money I so urgently needed. I was asked to help [for pay!] a professional dancing teacher with his classes — a request that was like throwing Brer Rabbit into the brier patch.)

6

When school opened that fall, I walked the four miles, with many misgivings; but not because I was still an Undesirable, for I now belonged. The Mayfield boys were my warm friends and gallant champions, furnishing an open sesame to the inner circle of Desirables. The misgivings that slowed my steps stemmed from rumors about the new teacher. He had been a successful teacher in "big schools," these rumors stated; but now he was growing blind and deaf and was on his way out. I felt sorry for him, I hope, but I wanted a Good Teacher.

How he filled that desire is one of the bright spots in my memories of school. From the minute I climbed over the freshly whitewashed stile onto the weedless school yard, saw the sparkling windows, and walked into the clean room, over which still hung a faint odor of Rub-No-More and water, my misgivings vanished. And when I saw the beautifully written "memory gems" on the board and

15

finally looked into the eyes of the elderly man who stood by his desk, my old Bug Scuffle excitement returned with all its force. Again I had found my ideal teacher!

It is true that some of the boys and girls at first took advantage of his infirmities, and created disturbances in the back of the room, but even they soon became so busy that they had little time to disturb. Here was the source of my fourth, fifth, and sixth precepts:

"Be ready for school before the opening day.

"Make plans for your work before school begins so that you will know where you are going and how you plan to get there.

"Keep your pupils busy and interested and you will have few discipline problems." These were expressed crudely in my *How To* book, but their meaning was plain.

Our lessons in penmanship were done in copybooks, in which we wrote, over and over, until the page was filled, at first brief but later longer inspirational quotations from literary masterpieces. Even yet when I am tempted to step on an ant, a bug, or a worm, I am stopped by Mr. Young's chiding "I would not enter on my list of friends a man who needlessly sets his foot upon a worm." All his messages, I thought, were meant just for me. One, especially, became both my inspiration and my goal:

> If a task is once begun,
> Never leave it till it's done;
> Be the labor great or small,
> Do it well or not at all.

I do not know who its composer was. Judged by standards of present critics, it may not even be called good poetry, but for me it "rang the bell." From the day I first

16

wrote it in my copybook until today, when it forces me
to write an autobiography, it has held me to difficult tasks
I was tempted to shirk; and it has compelled me to try to
do better some things that I might otherwise have done
carelessly. Presented by another teacher, the poem might
have been just a little rhyme; presented by my master
teacher, it became my lodestar for life.

This association soon led me to form my seventh precept: "A teacher has greater influence on a child's mind
and character than does any other individual in the whole
world. I must strive, therefore, to be worthy of this great
responsibility." Of course, I did not then know that I was
forming precepts; and naturally the terms I used to express
my convictions were not exactly like those used here, but
the ideas were there, and they grew. I rapidly developed
into a young idealist because my teacher was an idealist,
and I wanted to be just like him.

Just as England had her Golden Age in literature, so
had I my golden age. It covered my second and third years
in school — the last two years before Mr. Young became
totally blind and almost completely deaf. When I entered
school the second year, I had finished the second reader,
could spell most of the words in my older sisters' spellers,
could solve simple problems in arithmetic, but could hardly write a legible word. My teachers had listened as they
forced me to spell through my reading lessons, and that
was almost the extent of their teaching me. I had learned
to spell words through my own efforts, and had learned
combinations of numbers chiefly through observation of
other pupils' struggles.

My Mr. Young changed all this. He seemed to find

time to help everyone of us with everything. I read voraciously every book I could borrow or beg. I tried to improve my writing because Mr. Young wrote so beautifully, and it pleased him to see me improve. I worked harder toward the mastery of spelling because he praised me for my knowledge of words. I labored over the "tables" and other arithmetic problems because I could not let him know I was poor in any subject — though arithmetic was my "unfavorite" subject.

I wrote in my little book, "I just love Mr. Young. He makes me feel happy all the time."

Later, another of my guides as a result of this feeling became: "Take time to recognize effort, and to praise achievement, being sure every child has the opportunity to succeed in some activity. A child needs to experience success. He needs love and praise and a feeling of importance. I must not fail him."

Eager to learn everything, and consumed with the desire to win the approval of my teacher, my parents, and the Mayfields, I soon grew intensely interested in the history and geography lessons which the older students, seated on the recitation bench just in front of me, discussed with Mr. Young. Finally, I asked if I might recite with these older students. Though my sisters fumed and fussed and firmly refused me the use of their books, Papa bought me the books, and I began trotting up to the bench almost every time a new class was called.

But this was not the most important influence that came into my life through Mr. Young. He opened to me, in his short daily readings to the entire school, a completely new world. After he rang the bell (its call never seemed raucous in his hands) and we marched in and sang perhaps an old folk song or a church hymn, he read a passage to us from the Bible, often with his eyes closed. Then he took up a book, simple enough for the entire school to enjoy, and read us just one chapter. The book that almost drove me mad to hear what would happen next — it also kept Mama and Papa in a state of constant suspense for weeks — was *With Rex and Tawny, Fighting for the Lone Star State.* I took home each evening my version of that day's chapter, and no doubt the heroic exploits of Rex and Tawny, his horse, lost none of their miraculous flavor through my retelling the story.

Mr. Young also had a fifteen minute reading period at noon, beginning at 12:15. I would gobble my usual hard-boiled eggs, buttered bread, and fried apple pies or sugar pies and hurry to take my place in the magic group. No one was required to attend this reading period. It was only for those who loved reading; and at this period, the fare was much heavier. Selections from Scott, Byron, Keats, Wordsworth, Stevenson, Mark Twain, Poe, and the teacher's favorite — Shakespeare — were read in his rich, expressive voice.

Though the game of baseball that went on daily at noon outside had an almost irresistible appeal for me, and though I often understood little of what was being read, I was found each day with the small group of older students, mainly girls who disdained such rowdy sports as baseball and welcomed an opportunity to stay inside. When the reading was ended because the reader thought we should have some outdoor exercise, I dashed out to the baseball diamond and took my place as first baseman.

Toward the end of his second year with us (his last year of teaching) when Mr. Young was forced to give up his daily reading periods, those of us who loved the periods (and the reader) volunteered to read in his place. I am sure now this pleased him more than anything else we ever did while he taught us.

19

Every day was memorable in Mr. Young's school, but Friday afternoons were supreme. On those days our families and friends were invited to spend the afternoon listening to speaking, singing, and competition. On those occasions we delivered speeches; we had singsongs in which the whole assemblage joined, and we had arithmetic and spelling matches. I could never decide whether I liked best to recite a humorous piece, with all the mimicry I so enjoyed, or a serious piece, with all the extravagant gestures popular in that day. One week I was likely, therefore, to act our "Entertaining Sister's Beau"; the next I might, with up-flung arms, shout: "Give me liberty or give me death!"

But the event I loved best of all was the spelling match, which, like today's mile relay, was held last so that it could extend beyond four o'clock if necessary. Clint Mayfield and I were usually the last spellers left standing, and great was my elation when I could spell him down. Looking back on those contests now, I feel sure that he deliberately missed sometimes because he liked to see me happy, for he was older than I and a splendid student.

☆　　☆　　☆

By the time I had been in school three years, I did not belong to any particular grade; and not until I entered Cuero High School, at the age of fifteen, was I ever classified again. In the schools I attended I read, helped beginners and slow learners, and participated in or observed most of the advanced classes in reading, history, science, mathematics and grammar — one of my early favorites and still my most fascinating subject.

After my two golden years under Mr. Young's guidance, the succession of poor teachers we fell heir to could never dim my Dream. Instead, their shortcomings furnished much "fodder" for my *How To* book. One of these teachers, a frustrated old maid and a perfect model for all the old-maid-schoolteacher caricatures published before or since her time, had by Christmas so reduced her student body that for a time closing the school seemed eminent. When the county judge, who was also the county superintendent, sustained her contention that she should draw her salary whether she taught or not, the school was continued; but only a handful of students remained.

Among these few were all the members of my family then of school age — one of my older brothers, my younger sister, and I. All the other pupils had been driven from school by severe beatings for the weaker Undesirables or by permanent expulsion for the older boys, "Because," she charged, "they made ungentlemanly advances to me." ("Wishful thinking," my dad half-whispered to my mother when she brought home the story from a Ladies' Aid meeting.) Most of the older girls quit because the teacher forced them to suffer humiliating punishments for trivial or trumped-up offenses. Miss Irene filled many pages of my book with "How-Not-To's."

When she attempted to send my brother home one day (the enrollment then stood at eight out of more than thirty who had been enrolled), I was guilty of the only impudent behavior I ever exhibited at school. Leaving the board, where my brother had been explaining a problem to me (he was a math shark) I walked up close to her and calmly stated, "He is not going home, and none of the rest of us are going. You are paid to teach us, and you're going to teach us." All eight of us were in school when it closed late in April.

One other teacher furnished my little book with many observations. At the same time, he furnished us a school term of continuous frolic. As he was an inveterate reader, there were days when he took no notice of us at all, hearing not a single lesson all day. Our favorite activity on those days

21

was to catch, cook, and eat rabbits. Mr. Autrey sat near the door so none of us could leave without his seeing us; consequently we were forced to jump from the back window. First, two or three boys would go out and catch the cottontails, which were plentiful in that secluded area. Other boys would go out to prepare them for cooking; then the girls jumped out and took over the final preparations. The feast was usually enjoyed at recess, a period we had only because one of us would remind the teacher of the time.

No difficulty was encountered in entering the building at any time during one of his reading sprees. We simply walked in, said "Good morning, Mr. Autrey," received his mumbled "Good morning," and went to our seats. On the days when he decided to teach us he was really excellent; but his inability to control his reading addiction finally ruined his career as a teacher.

The only teacher I truly loved after Mr. Young was a little slip of brunette energy, who came to school every day looking — to use a popular cliché of that day — "as though she had just stepped out of a bandbox." She knew her subject matter; she understood and loved her raw materials; she had a glorious sense of humor; and she could hold her own with the best of us in games on the playground. Yet, when the occasion demanded, she could quell an obstreperous yokel who respected only force with the only control he understood. For me it was love at first sight, and many Miss-Susie-inspired entries in my book helped me in my early days of teaching.

7

We had by this time traded our abandoned, worn-out ranch in Karnes County for a small river-bottom farm in

De Witt County and had opened a small country store in Concrete, Texas. I now attended a three-teacher school so modern that the building was painted, though the only library we had was a large dictionary that lacked its cover and many of its pages.

We had moved away from my Mrs. Mayfield, with her music, her dancing, her flowers on the table at meals, and her books; and my Mr. Young, now totally blind, had gone to live with his sister. Now the only reading material available to me other than my textbooks, which were not yet furnished by the state, was *Comfort,* a monthly magazine that cost twenty-five cents a year, and the *Galveston Semi-Weekly News,* a must for Papa's happiness. How I pored over the pages of *Comfort,* reading avidly the somewhat colorless stories, reveling in Uncle Charlie's page, and, when these were sucked dry, carefully studying every advertisement! One of these puzzled me no end. It carried a picture of some queer-looking straps and advised people who were "Ruptured" to "Wear This Truss!" I had asked my older sister what it meant, but she was so scandalized that I did not have the temerity to pursue the inquiry further.

The *Semi-Weekly News* had my same devoted perusal as did *Comfort,* and it was my interest in these periodicals that incited my first attempts at writing for publication. The *News* had a page devoted to letters from its subscribers, and I became one of its frequent contributors. Since the two most controversial issues of the day were Prohibition and Woman's Suffrage, I became a Carrie Nation and a Susan B. Anthony rolled into one. It did not occur to me that my age, experience, and knowledge were such as made my opinions worthless. I had most dogmatic convictions on both subjects and a yen to express them.

The letter I wrote to *Galveston Semi-Weekly News* on the evils of alcohol was a tearjerker of the first water, for I had observed the effect of this "dread curse" on a fine family living near us, and I spared no details to make my letter convincing. My patient, indulgent, and usually admiring dad, who never struck any of his children, no matter what their misdeeds, almost took me out to the woodshed when the letter appeared with its extremely personal and all-too-true details. I had used everything but names of the family. Even now I do not know what sense of delicacy caused me to omit these.

As the result of this letter I was swamped with fan mail — the first ever to come to our community — and from the doghouse of condemnation for poor taste, I was elevated to a pinnacle of fame. I was now an eminent writer!

I wish I could quote the story of our alcoholic neighbor as I wrote it for the *News*. Memory dims, however, after many years. This is a recast of my story as I vividly remember the events if not the exact words in my *News* letter.

Just up the street from us — well, really just a dusty road — lived a blacksmith and his frail but indomitable little wizened wife.

Each Saturday Mr. Smith hitched his rawboned old white mare to his equally rawboned buggy and took off for his weekly ten-mile trip to town. (I interrupt here to say that the old mare "upped and died" one day from an overdose of arsenic which had been administered by Mr. Smith in preparation for Trade's Day that Saturday. The arsenic was to puff her up as if she were fat. In his enthusiasm he had overdone it.)

Now, back to my story — Invariably Mr. Smith topped the low hill just west of our store, singing to the top of his voice, "Amazing Grace" on his way home from town. My brother and I knew this meant we would soon be picking up a strew of bolts from the dusty road, for Mr. Smith always stopped by our store and bought a box of bolts — the same box each Saturday — and charged them. These he scattered along the road only a short distance from our home and store. As a consequence my brother and I had to pick up the bolts and return them to our

24

store, to be sold again and charged (never paid for) the next Saturday.

Late one afternoon when we had again picked up the bolts and were out at the barn with Papa, we heard a loud commotion coming from the Smith house. Screams for help, curses, pleas!

Papa sent us scurrying to the Smith house to find the source of the trouble. There we found Mrs. Smith placidly rocking away on her little front porch, while the pleas for help came from behind the house. She told us, without change of voice or expression, or even change of rhythm in her rocking: "He's down in the cistern. The durned old fool is drunk as usual. He keeps his jug down in the cistern so I can't destroy it. Well, I just up and took out his ladder. When he started down, he went down in a hurry. Let him stay down there. There ain't no water."

By this time Papa had arrived, and replacing the ladder, he went down and helped the old fellow out. This was the story I told in my famous *News* letter. Sadly both Mr. Smith and his wife were educated people from a cultured family. Fortunately they had no children nor any close relatives.

This success as an author and my intense sympathy for Uncle Charlie, a cripple who edited a page of letters, poems, and essays in *Comfort*, inspired my next "great literary achievement," for now I must write to Uncle Charlie. Trying to comfort him, I am afraid I hinted that he should be thankful he was just a cripple confined to his bed, where at least he could rest, and not a poor underprivileged Woman in America, or a Slave to the Insidious Snares of Demon Liquor, or — worse than either — the Child of a Cotton Farmer in the Barren South — a poor, toil-worn, stoop-shouldered child dragging a heavy sack under a blistering sun or endlessly swinging a hoe.

Though I stood as straight as an unbent cottonwood sapling and actually had unusual freedoms, I sometimes led myself to believe that I had been the inspiration for Edwin Markham's "The Man with the Hoe":

> Bowed by the weight of centuries, he leans
> Upon his hoe and gazes on the ground,
> The emptiness of ages on his face
> And on his back the burden of the world.

Markham's own explanation of the poem, which I found years later in an anthology of American literature, expressed what I would have said, I believe, if I had known how:[1]

> The Yeoman is the landed and well-to-do farmer; you need shed no tears for him. But here in the Millet picture is the opposite — the Hoeman: the landless, the soul-blighted workman of the world; the dumb creature that has no time to rest, no time to think, no time for the hopes that make us men.

To show Uncle Charlie the sad lot of a cotton farmer's child, I even resorted to a poem of my own. By this time I had received such acclaim (I thought) for my masterpiece on alcohol, that I imagined myself a young Joan of Arc, with an evangelistic urge to root out the major evils of society. When Uncle Charlie published my letter and poem and added indignant comments of his own about the sad plight of the poor overworked children of the South, my fame became unassailable, but my popularity with the older generation suffered an eclipse.

Though my *How To* book and my treasured scrapbook, which held these literary successes, were destroyed recently by an illiterate Negro woman employed to assist me in housecleaning, this is my poem, as nearly as I can recall it:

---

[1] Rewey B. Inglis, *et al.*, *Adventures in American Literature*, 1949, 757.

26

King Cotton, creator of slaves,
I Hate you! I Hate you, I Hate you!
Your beauty like a banner waves,
But still I hate you.
For hidden in those blossoms white,
And sheltered 'neath that foliage
    green,
Is bitter toil that lurks unseen.
O how I hate you!

With young backs bowed and fingers
    raw,
Your weary dupes their burdens draw;
With Children's dreams you glut
    your maw.[2]
I hate you! How I hate you!

But I will never be your slave;
No sweat of mine your roots
    shall lave.
I'll brush your lint out of my
    hair;
I'll see you rot and never care;
Go now and seek some weaker fare —
Or rot — alone in your despair.
No matter now how you behave,
I'll Always Hate You!

If Walt Whitman could take liberties with versification
and rhyme scheme, why should I hesitate!

8

I was nearly thirteen at this time, and for more than a

---

2 I had just met *Beowulf*.

year after these glowing successes, I was willing to rest on my laurels, perhaps because so many other fascinating interests had come into my life; and, like most reformers who had changed from the status of Have-nots to Haves, I was too happy to spend much time reforming. My dad had recovered, and our financial condition had improved to such an extent that we now had a telephone. We had owned an Edison phonograph for some time. (I can still hear it playing "You're as Welcome as the Flowers in May.") And the most wonderful of all our possessions was parked out in the shed, a descendant, or maybe even a twin brother, to the vision I had failed to catch one Sunday morning after church — a gorgeous red Reo automobile. The fact that it was secondhand and often refused to run detracted not one whit from its splendor, nor from our social standing in the community. We had arrived.

☆ ☆ ☆

These were not the most important interests in my life at the time, however. I had become first baseman on the community baseball team made up entirely of men and boys — except me. And I had fallen completely in love with a most daring, reckless, utterly fascinating young man, sixteen years old! While these interests occupied my every thought, I forgot that the world needed a reformer like me, and I almost discarded my dream of being a teacher. When one day, seeking to find a safe place to hide my love notes from the prying eyes of my sisters and brothers, I came upon my *How to Teach School* book, my dream came back to me, as powerful as ever.

Almost immediately my beau and his big red Ranger bicycle and his beautiful black pony, on which I could fly down the country lanes, lost their powerful charms — though I wept bitterly when I returned his wishbone stickpin and told him, "I just don't love you enough," in what I imagined was an Elizabeth Barrett Browning voice.

It required an even greater struggle for me to give up my secret dream of being the first woman to play big league baseball. *How To* won, however, and I spent my last year in the little rural school, studying with feverish interest and adding many new observations to my book. I could hardly wait until I became sixteen and could begin my life's work.

9

With the desire to prepare to teach paramount in my mind, in September after I was fifteen in August, I entered high school, where I was subjected to a week of tests before I was classified as a senior. I was woefully weak in higher math and had had no foreign language, a requisite then for graduation; but my grades in history, science, and especially literature and grammar were the deciding factors in my favor. I was finally a senior, with graduation in prospect in the spring — if I could do two years' work in German in one year. Fraulein Mauer, a visiting teacher from Germany, gave me many outside hours of help so that I could do in a few weeks the work required in first-year German and thus catch up with the second-year German class before midterm.

On the opening day of high school, our English class was thrown into a flurry by the announcement of a literary contest whose winner would receive ten dollars! "To encourage the Fine Arts," the Turkey Trot committee would award a blue ribbon and ten dollars to the high school student in De Witt County (which contained Cuero, Yoakum, and Yorktown High Schools, as well as innumerable rural schools) who wrote the best essay on some literary masterpiece. I pondered earnestly over my choices of a subject but finally settled on Coleridge's *Rime of the Ancient Mariner.* When the winning essay, with a blue ribbon pinned to it and ten enormous silver dollars stacked beside it, was placed in the glass exhibit case at the fairgrounds, my name — Cleo Winslett — looked almost as wonderful on its cover as did the ten dollars beside it. Every day as long as the Turkey Trot, (an annual De Witt County Fair held in Cuero) lasted, I hung over the case to reassure myself that I had not dreamed it all.

In spite of the fact that I had to acquire two credits of German in one year, solve the intricacies of the use of library books and references, and worry each week for fear my family could not pay my board and tuition (another flood had struck with its consequent ruin of crops and loss at the store), I was hoping to graduate with honors. Then I was stricken with typhoid fever. To me it seemed that my hopes were shattered forever before I was sixteen. Such is the devastating effect of disappointment on youth. Perhaps the ravages of typhoid contributed to my hopeless despair too.

Again my faith in the teaching profession was forever established when my teachers unanimously petitioned the superintendent and the school board to grant my diploma. The night it was brought out to me (I was still too weak to be up) was one of the happiest in my entire life. My brother proudly made a frame for it the next day and hung it at the foot of my bed, where it apparently furnished the medicine I needed, for my recovery after that night was miraculous.

10

It seemed that my long-suffering family lived through

one crisis with me, only to be subjected to another. Hardly had I begun to get about with some of my old strength and enthusiasm, and certainly before the financial strain resulting from my year in high school and my expensive illness had lessened, when I learned that a Summer Normal was to be held in Cuero that summer and that I could obtain a teacher's certificate if I would attend and then pass the examinations at the end of the term. I just had to go — but how? I still had the ten silver dollars my essay had won at the Turkey Trot. I owned a young cow and her calf — offspring of a jersey heifer given to a little ten-year-old girl for cooking and serving "the best meal we have ever eaten" for my father and three businessmen from town when my mother was not at home. And I could do without any new clothes — they were not important anyway.

Having sold my livestock to pay the matriculation fee, buy my books and pay my board, and having been supplied with a few new clothes my mother had managed to make for me — she was a genius at making beautiful things from practically nothing — I set off very early one Monday morning in search of my Holy Grail — a Teacher's Certificate. For the first time in my life, I was really scared. "Suppose I can't pass," I thought. "Suppose I can't get a certificate at all!" I was in a state of complete panic when Papa, having deposited my little trunk at Mrs. Burdick's, where I had lived in the winter, deposited me at the high school — site of the normal.

We were expected to pass examinations in fourteen subjects: English; Texas, United States, ancient, and medieval histories; arithmetic, geography, physiology, general science, agriculture, the history of education, methods and management, and (I think but am not sure) elementary psychology. I decided that I would outline every lesson every day and so be ready to review at the end of the term. I found the task herculean and all but impossible to accomplish; the days and nights were just not long enough.

Besides, I was tempted by offers of dates made by attractive boys, invitations to attend the movies (a luxury I could not afford) with girls I liked, and my longing to attend exciting baseball games, played almost daily all summer. When I decided to abandon my self-imposed study plan, since no one else in school felt such work necessary, my lodestar — "If a task is once begun" — held me to my exacting labor. And when results of the examinations were announced, and less than twenty-five percent of the summer students were granted teacher's certificates, I knew I had Mr. Young to thank for mine.

☆　☆　☆

Finally when the normal ended about the middle of August, and I went home with the promise of a job in a little one-teacher school — if I got my certificate — I found our fields white with cotton and no pickers to be found anywhere. When before sunrise the next morning, I saw my two younger sisters and my little seven-year-old brother start out to help in the field, I put on old clothes, picked up a despised cotton sack (an act I had vowed never again to perform), and went out to struggle again with my loathsome enemy. If my intense hatred for cotton could have increased, it would have done so as my fingers bled from the prickly cotton bolls and my legs became "stringhalted" from bending so long.

It was in the cotton patch under a blistering late August sun that my certificate was brought to me by our excited mail carrier, who, knowing my extreme anxiety, had left his route and brought the thickly padded envelope with its return address: Department of Education, Austin, Texas. When I saw that it was really mine and the highest granted for this type of work — a certificate for six years — I sat down and wept as I had not wept since, as a little seven-year-old in another cotton patch, I thought I could not start to school.

☆　☆　☆

My family's pride and joy over my success were the sweetest rewards I had ever enjoyed, not excluding my ten-dollar prize nor my fame as a writer for publication. All of us promptly took our sacks to the wagon and went to the house to celebrate. I sat down at my organ — a gift from my favorite uncle — and struck up "Praise God from Whom All Blessings Flow" while everybody sang. Then "Where the River Shannon Flows," "Where the Silvery Colorado Wends Its Way," "Red Wing," "Red River Valley," and even "Sweet Adeline" were sung with more volume than harmony. Mama, never idle, had slipped off to whip up hot gingerbread, and this, with cold clabber from a bucket in the well, furnished our refreshments, so delicious the gods would have disdained their choicest nectar for such fare.

Then Mama and Papa, suddenly remembering some pressing church business, dashed off in the buggy — the Reo was enjoying one of its balky periods — and went to spread the good news among our friends.

PART TWO

Never Leave It Till
It's Done

1

The days following the arrival of my certificate were filled with feverish excitement and bustling activity. I must spend the next week in Cuero at Teachers' Institute, a sort of orientation, inspiration, and "socialization" period for all the teachers of the county.

To camouflage my extreme youth and to take care of an overdue need, Mama and I spent the next day in town, where we bought the first ready-made dresses I had ever owned. Previously even my coats had been made at home. A blue-gray, intricately draped hobble skirt and a never-to-be-forgotten dull gold "afternoon dress" made up my ready-made wardrobe. To set these off, we bought a black plush hat with a crushed band and huge bow of black faille interwoven with gold cord-like threads. My shoes were black patent with high-buttoned tops of black kid — the last word in elegance. We were at that time again in the money, for it was cotton-picking time and prices were up because of the war that had broken out in Europe.

Advised by my Miss Susie, who was now married and living near us, we also bought material for my first evening gown, for we had been told that on the last night of Institute a "Formal Reception and Ball," in the Mohawk Club Rooms, would top off all the social activities of the week in which we were dined but never wined. We planned to splurge and buy a ready-made formal, but prices in this line staggered us. We therefore looked all the formals over, made mental notes of the things we liked about each, then went home for Mama to make one more beautiful than any other dress in the entire world. It was made of heavy, rustly, forest green taffeta. Scalloped at the hem and at the bouffant hip line with a deep, petal-shaped design outlined with narrow double ruffles of the same petal-shaped scallops. It would have been considered immodestly revealing had it not had a soft, cream-colored lace "guimpe," with very full short puffed sleeves.

On the night of the ball, when I reverently slipped into this dream-dress, pinned my usually unrestrained curls high on my head, and perched upon them a forest green taffeta bow, I knew I was ready to conquer the world.

Clothes may not make the man, but they certainly make the woman — that is, they make her enjoy a self-confidence that nothing else can give. As the glamorous young beaus vied for my program on which to write their names for a dance, and as I floated over the fairy dance floor to the strains of Raphael's Mexican String Band, life was a sublime joy.

One of the young Mohawk Club members, who wrote his name on my program and then asked me to sit out the number since he did not dance, had a vast influence on my life. He later became the Number One Man for me — my husband.

That night, however, I could hardly endure the loss of this one dance, particularly as it was (next to "Over the Waves") my favorite waltz — "Let Me Call You Sweetheart." The fact that the man with whom I sat sang the words to me in a most romantic and truly good voice did not impress me at the time. I was only glad my program was filled so that this non-dancer could claim no more of my time, as he seemed determined to do.

☆　　☆　　☆

The Institute had been a week of absolute bliss for me. A barely sixteen-year-old idealist about to realize my dream at last, I drank in every inspirational message, took copious notes on all lectures, pestered experienced teachers about teaching, invested most of the money Papa had given me to spend — as I pleased — in "flash cards," "reading games," and other "teacher's aids," and reveled in my prestige as a teacher and in the social activities with which we were entertained. Teachers really occupied a bright spot in the sun in those halcyon days.

My early training in spelling matches helped me to become the fair-haired lass of that Institute. On Monday night following the day Institute convened, the round of entertainment which we were to enjoy that week was opened with a watermelon party at the home of a member of our State Legislature, who was also editor of the *Cuero Star,* a weekly newspaper. The businessmen in town were hosts for the party. The big event of the evening was a spelling match in which the teachers were pitted against the businessmen. Some of the teachers "didn't feel like spelling," and some of the men were afflicted with the same ailment. Though I had more than a touch of it myself, with fear in my heart, I took my place near the end of the line of healthier members of our profession.

The match was long and exciting as the two sides battled it out. Finally, however, only three of us were left — my senior high school English teacher, Mr. Crisp and I. When my teacher went out on *asafoetida,* and then Mr. Crisp put the *e* before *u* in *Portuguese,* I knew I had won. Again I had Mr. Young to thank for my success, for it was he who had first introduced me to *Sonnets from the Portuguese* as well as to the joy of competitive spelling.

I became the toast of the Institute, for I had vindicated the reputation of the teaching profession by defeating the

39

man who knew more about words than did any other in the community — a man who had already taken up the hue and cry which was to increase to such proportions (and justly so) — "Schools are not teaching children to spell."

2

The days between the close of Institute and the first Monday in October rushed by like a runaway team frightened by the sight of its first train, and I rushed just as blindly. Each day in my frenzy of studying, planning, packing, and re-packing, I was troubled with misgivings, only vague at first. These soon, however, changed to doubt, then to dread and fear. I would think of my family's pride and confidence; I would remember my unfulfilled dream; and I would wonder if I were equal to the task I was about to attempt.

Though I would gladly have suspended the calendar and stopped the clock, the day I was to go out to Rosebud Community, where my job awaited me, hurtled inevitably nearer. My dad and I, consequently, arose before dawn one Saturday morning and drove to Cuero to meet Mr. Parker, the "big wheel" of Rosebud School. He had insisted that he would meet me in Cuero, though Papa really wanted to take me all the way to my boarding place himself.

Mr. Parker was old. Everything about him was old — his sunken gray eyes; his billiard-ball head with its fringe of scanty, white hair; his shrunken gums, to which only a few tobacco-stained teeth clung; his long gray whiskers that spread like a bib over his vest; his rusty, green-black suit; his upstanding age-yellow celluloid collar with its two sharp turned-down points lost under his whiskers — his very being emanating antiquity and stagnancy — and self-complacency!

As he crawled from his equally ancient buggy and enveloped my trembling hand in his twisted, brown-splotched fist, I was tempted to run to my dad and plead, "Let's go back home."

The quiet pride with which Papa stood by and watched me, however, restored my courage. Instead of retreat, I forced myself to say, "Here are my things. Where shall we put them?"

"Why am I afraid?" I asked myself. "Now the great day is almost here — the day toward which I have been building for nine years: I am going out to teach school!"

My little brown trunk, secured with strands of farm-worn rope, sat on the back of the ancient buggy, covering the space usually occupied by the week's supply of food and other farm necessities. To make room for the trunk and the small suitcase tucked into the space under it, these supplies had been piled up on the floor of the buggy.

As, with extreme difficulty, I placed my foot on the buggy step, and then pulled myself into the worn seat on the left hand of the driver, I wondered where I could find rest for my suffering feet. Still ringing in my ears was Mama's injunction — "Be dignified" — yet how could I achieve a feeling of dignity, to say nothing of a look of dignity, with my feet propped high on a jug of molasses? How could I feel even self-respect, all dressed up like a plush horse in a long, horrible, freedom-destroying hobble skirt and a stiff white shirtwaist, which had already "taken the hide off" the area around my neck and ears?

The weight of the world, which had settled on my chest early that morning when I left home with Papa to meet this formidable trustee, increased unbearably as I looked at the set smile of Papa's usually gay face and saw the difficulty with which he was trying to swallow.

Suddenly I felt terribly alone, utterly lost, and horribly scared. And my too-new, high-heeled, high-topped button shoes, planted precariously on top of a sticky jug of molasses, which in turn was perched on a large package of Arbuckle's coffee, added to my torture, for they were inflicting indescribable agony on hitherto almost unconfined, frankly-large feet.

If one must suffer to be elegant, as Mrs. Wiggs of the Cabbage Patch would have us believe, and if the amount of suffering is an indication of the degree of elegance, that day I was the most elegant of all the people who inhabit the earth. I did not desire elegance, however, nor did I particularly desire dignity. I was following a childhood Dream. I wanted above everything else to be a schoolteacher — a good schoolteacher!

But here I sat in this uncomfortable position beside a strange, stern man — a man as old as time itself — on whom, I had been warned, my future as a teacher depended. Here I sat with a wobbly smile on my face, looking at Papa and wondering, in my desperate homesickness, why I had ever thought I wanted to leave home.

I had ample time to ponder on bits of advice and parting injunctions from my family and even on the tragedy of having to grow up and conform to a prescribed social pattern, as the old gray mare, never exceeding a slow walk, plodded the long six miles from Cuero to Rosebud. And while Mr. Parker, my garrulous driver, who had insisted that he meet me in Cuero so he could let me know early what he expected of me, talked and chewed his tobacco and talked some more, I sat heartsick and utterly forlorn.

The candid old codger, who I soon learned was patriarch of his little community and was consequently the most influential of its three school trustees, certainly did nothing to encourage me or banish my despair when he bluntly informed me he had opposed hiring me. "Why, you ain't dry behind the ears yet," he blurted out, glaring at me over his steel-rimmed glasses. And to this day, I shudder when I hear that crude expression.

He spent the interminable drive telling me that I was too young for the job; that I could never control the pupils, some of whom were several years older than I; and

42

that it was almost impossible for one so inexperienced to resist the temptations and evade the evils and dangers in the community. While I sat and suffered and listened to his endless monologue, I longed to drop a giant firecracker under the plodding old mare.

"Hold that temper, Cleo," I could almost hear my mother say. "My precious, hard-working, wonderful mother," I thought. "I must justify her belief in me."

As a concession to her firm conviction that a girl could never quite be a lady until she dressed the part, I sat in those impossible clothes, with the misery of discomfort added to that of fear, homesickness, and despair. The intolerably tight shoes (ladies should have small feet); the long, narrow action-restricting skirt; the refined shirtwaist, with its stiff collar and cuffs — a fit successor to the Puritan stocks or the pillory — all these were the result of Mama's hope that at last she could turn her tomboy daughter into a lady. To please her further, I had piled my unruly hair on top of my head and fastened it there with hairpins and "side combs." On this topknot I had perched a cartwheel straw hat and secured it there with two long black-headed hat pins, for ladies must wear hats, not travel bareheaded.

So there I sat in those conventional, absurd shackles, partly to please Mama and partly to try to look like a grown-up lady, a lady old enough to teach school. Snatches of my family's parting injunctions vied in my mind with Mr. Parker's gloomy semi-soliloquy.

"Be a lady," Mama had implored.

"Smile at them kids and they'll love you," had come from John Hennessee, our hired man who was as much a part of the family as I, having been a member even before my time.

"Just be yourself, Daughter," had been Papa's sound advice.

And, "Give 'em hell!" had been whispered by my brother just older than I, who was quite a man, courting the girls, smoking an occasional cigarette filched from John's private stock of Bull Durham, and "cussing" a bit if he was sure neither Mama nor Papa could hear him.

All these bits of advice occupied my thoughts as Mr. Parker carried on his uninterrupted, eternal monologue. Thinking of what a delight it would be to use my brother's advice right there, I shifted my feet from the molasses jug to the five-gallon can of kerosene and, in the shift, clumsily knocked off the potato which acted as a stopper on the spout. Out "sloshed" the kerosene all over my lady-shoes and the groceries in the box. After a frantic but fruitless attempt to repair the damage, I stammered inanely, "I didn't quite hear what you were just saying."

Mr. Parker merely looked at me with contempt and disgust, then spit a stream of tobacco juice intended for the dusty roadside. Some of it did reach its intended destination. Some, however, made a rich brown stream down his long gray whiskers; and not a few brown, breeze-blown flecks landed on my white shirtwaist.

"Be a lady," I was forced to remind myself as the "living lightning flashed from out" my eyes. Angry as I was, however, I knew I must not put into practice here my brother's advice, though I longed to do just that.

"Well, we're might near there," he finally announced. "It ain't a very comfortable place, but the eatin's good, and you probably won't be here very long anyway."

These last words were the boost I needed to pull me out of my slough of despair. All the pugnacity of generations of Irish ancestors, all the hard-headedness of every Scotch forefather, all the unconquerable Welsh blood in my being made me resolve that I would stay in Rosebud and teach that school. In spite of — no, I could not say "hell and high water"; that would be unladylike — but anyway, here I would stay.

"Just smile at them kids," the hired man had advised. Why wouldn't that work on Mr. Parker? So calling on all the self-control, acting ability, and charm I possessed, I

44

turned to him as he came to a gate that opened into a short, dusty lane leading to the large, shabby old house where I was to board. I looked him straight in the eyes, smiled my ingenuous, friendly smile — not the one my brother called my Cleopatra smile — and said, "I'll still be here, Mr. Parker, when school closes next spring."

3

Though the sun shone brightly on the morning I was to begin the realization of my great Dream, it held no brightness for me. My Dream had become a terrible nightmare, and I awoke in a state of utter panic. My first thought was that I would call Papa to come and take me home. Then I remembered my promise to Mr. Parker. I would not admit defeat. I *would* be there when school closed next spring.

Somehow, I put on the gray hobble skirt and a severely plain shirtwaist (but I could not resist tying a bright red bow under my chin). Then I slicked my curls down and rolled them into two knots, which I pinned securely, one over each ear. But in spite of my efforts to look mature, when I tried to get some breakfast past the knot in my throat, Ed, the dour old bachelor son in the Teller family, increased my panic by telling me I looked like a little girl playing lady. Hastily snatching up my lunch basket, I hobbled off down the sandy lane to school — that day a short mile away.

I had planned to reach school early so that I could have time to compose myself and be ready when the first pupil arrived. Imagine my horror, therefore, when I came in sight of school and saw a school yard full of boys and girls, though it was only seven-thirty.

My consternation was complete when I entered the building and found Mr. Parker and the two other trustees sitting near my desk calmly awaiting my arrival. One of the three trustees was a young fellow with only a preschool-age child. Another was a Mr. Krause, a thrifty German farmer, with a heart of gold, and ten children, seven of whom were now in the school yard. Mr. Parker, the man who had contributed to my nightmare, had married a widow much younger than he (and she was not young) and was the very proud stepfather of a thirty-five-year-old son, who proved much harder for me to handle than did his father.

By the cat-that-ate-the-canary look in Mr. Parker's eyes, and the uncomfortable appearance of Mr. Bennett and Mr. Krause, I knew whose brain had fathered the idea of their visit to the school. This knowledge gave me the impetus I so needed to take me through the day, for it made me furious and stubbornly determined to succeed. Before the day ended, I had need of all the stubborn courage I could muster, for those three trustees — with time out only to answer the call of nature, or, in the case of Mr. Parker, to bring in a forgotten can in which to eject his tobacco juice — sat right on that rostrum in three stiff-backed chairs and watched my every move until I dismissed school at four o'clock. I felt their eyes glued to my back when I rang the bell to assemble the students. Like vultures the solemn three sat in utter silence while we sang our morning song and while we read in unison the Twenty-Third Psalm, which I had placed on the board on Sunday. They bowed their heads but kept their eyes trained on me, I felt, as we repeated The Lord's Prayer together. They sat on and on until I longed to do some shocking thing that would send them (and me) home.

Later when Mr. Bennett had become my tower of strength and Mr. Krause had become my warm personal adviser and friend, we laughed about that miserable day, and they confirmed what I had suspected: They were just as

46

uncomfortable as I. Having been newly-elected that spring as trustees, they had deferred to Mr. Parker's wishes; but during that long day, they came to the conclusion that it was time for the Parker rule to cease.

A tiny Mexican boy named Peter, accompanied by his English-speaking father and his cousin Joe, a tall, well-built, fifteen-year-old, created the big crisis on my first day. When they arrived about two o'clock and the father asked me to enroll them in school, Mr. Parker arose and firmly announced:

"Mescans ain't allowed in this here school. It's jist fer whites."

Calmly I invited them to sit down (my invitation was repeated by the two other trustees) and, ignoring Mr. Parker, I enrolled the two in the first grade. Before the school year ended, that act paid big dividends for me.

Somehow, four o'clock finally came, and the children and trustees left me to the quiet of the empty schoolroom, where I worked until daylight began to fade, rearranging my daily schedule and setting the building in order. As I hurried home, I was met by Ed, who, alarmed at my failure to come home, had come to look for me. It was hard to keep back the tears when I saw him coming down the lane.

"You can't do it all in one day, girl," he chided me as I gratefully took my place in the buggy.

4

The kindness and genuine friendliness of that German family, composed of a widow and her middle-aged son and daughter, were sources of much comfort to me. The meals they served, including my cold lunches, were consistently the best I have ever eaten. My bedroom was simple and almost bare of furnishings but it was spotless, as was the entire house. For this comfort I paid ten dollars per calendar month, and the family did my laundry. This was

47

in keeping with my salary, however, which was forty-nine dollars and seventy-five cents per month. This figure was arrived at by dividing the total available school funds — $348.25 — into seven equal parts, and I was paid one of these parts each month. Supplies for the school such as wood, chalk, an occasional broom and rare repairs on the building were provided by the community, usually the trustees.

When I received my first month's pay, I was rich beyond measure. But after I had paid my board, bought a dictionary for the school, subscribed for *St. Nicholas* that my children might have one magazine to read, and bought my dad a handsome gray suit for fifteen dollars and my mother materials for a silk dress, I was almost without funds again. Since this was no novelty to me, it caused me no particular worry. I needed little cash either for necessities or for happiness.

As the busy days passed, I found teaching more wonderful than even my fondest dream had pictured it. To help the little Have-Nots grow more self-confident and happy and the Haves grow kinder and more democratic, to see the rapid development of my two Mexican protégés, Peter and Joe — the first of their race ever to attend Rosebud School for more than a day or two — and to feel that my pupils trusted me and wanted to learn — all these were the intangible income that supplemented my small monthly salary.

My students ranged in age from seven to twenty. I had three boys and several girls older than I.

At that time my pet hate was tobacco chewing, a dislike that had been intensified when, on that interminable ride

48

out from town, some of Mr. Parker's amber-colored spittle, intended for the roadside, had landed on me instead. Consequently, when we came to a study of the ill effects of nicotine on the human body, I went all out to do battle against this particular evil.

One day, after what I thought was an especially effective lesson, one of the older boys — a dull-witted, overgrown nineteen-year-old arose, kissed his plug of Brown Mule, deposited it on my desk, and pledged himself never to use the Filthy Weed again. Great was my elation until on Friday he lingered after school and asked me for a date that night for the usual weekly dance held on Friday nights at school. It was then I realized it was only to impress his teacher and not to protect his health that he had kissed his plug good-bye.

5

The crushes of my pupils I could turn aside and still retain their friendship, but the annoying attention of Mr. Parker's obnoxious stepson was my special cross-I-had-to-bear, for he fancied himself a combination Romeo, Lothario, and Casanova and chose me as his Juliet. A college graduate, an indolent dude and ladykiller of the first water, and the apple of his stepfather's eye, he made my life miserable for months, much more miserable than his stepfather could make it.

When I got to school mornings, I found passionate love notes and romantic bouquets of flowers on my desk; when I started home in the late afternoon, or early afternoon or any other time, it seemed, he was sure to be waiting at the school yard gate, in his fancy rig — a red-wheeled, rubber-tired buggy drawn by a fast-stepping bay. Thinking to discourage him, I assured him I liked to walk home for exercise; but the next day, mounted on his bay, he waited at the gate to insist upon walking home with me and leading his horse.

Since I had little experience in the field of courtship, and none where such an "elderly" man was involved, I became desperate for a way out. Fate, in the guise of a black cat, finally furnished me the means for getting rid of him without resorting to some drastic measure.

He made a date to take me to a box supper and dance at school, and it was important that I be there early to get things ready for the school program that was to start off the evening's fun. Mrs. Teller and Elsie and Ed went on, leaving me dressed and sitting on the porch, impatiently waiting for the obnoxious Henry. When I saw him drive through the gate from the lane, then turn around and drive away, I was puzzled and furious. Taking my gaily decorated heart-shaped box, which was filled with Mrs. Teller's best foods, I started off in all my finery down the sandy, weed-bordered lane toward school.

When time for the program came and I had not appeared, Ed, my faithful watchdog, came to look for me and bring me on to take care of the delayed program. I was in a cold, quiet, but absolute rage, which did not lessen when I learned the reason for Henry's unusual behavior. Just as he had driven through the gate, a black cat had crossed the driveway leading to the house, where I waited on the porch. Fearing to continue when a black cat had crossed his path and so bring down disaster upon himself, he had turned his horse and rushed back home to telephone me and ask me to be patient while he made a fresh start. But I had not waited for his call.

This furnished me a long-desired opportunity, and I made the most of it. That I was irreparably humiliated and inconsolably offended was the attitude I assumed, and the sympathy of the entire assemblage agreed with me when I absolutely refused to eat with him after he had paid ten dollars for my box. One of my masculine sympathizers, realizing the situation, ran the bidding up that high.

Neither would I dance with him nor permit him to make peace with me in any way. I had a rare old time dramatizing my deep injury and secretly blessing the black cat which had so opportunely helped me get rid of a pest.

6

My work up to the Christmas holidays seemed entirely satisfactory to the community. I was no marvel, and some of my teaching techniques were antediluvian, I am afraid. My deficiencies here, however, were somewhat alleviated by my enthusiasm, boundless energy, interest in people, and love for my work. Nothing that would improve my students was too much work. So I was able to organize, control, and hold classes for thirty-eight pupils; and I was not once forced to resort to the rawhide buggy whip that Henry had given me the first week of school. He was afraid, he had explained, that I would need protection against the big boys who had caused the last teacher at Rosebud before me to look for a more pleasant occupation than teaching. During these weeks a study of my *How To* book was of invaluable help and comfort to me.

One of the things it recalled to my mind was how much children love a teacher who plays. One day, therefore, after I had forgotten the restraint of my tight, long skirt and jumped off Mr. Bennett's front porch, landing on my head on the hard-packed ground and splitting my skirt from ankle to knee, I hung my grown-up clothes behind the bright chintz curtain that protected my clothes in my prim, bare room at Mrs. Teller's and went back to the comfortable pleated skirts and middy blouses of my high school days, and to my place at first base (a place I had to earn, incidentally) in the daily ball games at school.

From the day I discarded my finery and became one of them, my stock began to soar. When I began to play with them on the school ground, they were much more willing to "play ball" with me in the schoolroom.

"Gee Whizz!" an ugly little toughie whose one aim in life was to become a big-time baseball player shouted. "Gee Whizz Golly! I didn't know a teacher could hit a ball like that!" I had just tagged home base after knocking an easy pitch over the bushes outside the school yard fence.

It was my observation then, and it is still my firm conviction, that the teacher who is interested in the games, sports, and social life of her pupils and takes time to play with them is a more successful teacher than one who dwells in an ivory tower.

☆　　☆　　☆

If I were to advance any other reasons for the fact that I was able to defy the pioneer philosophy, "No lickin', no larnin'," still a prevalent conviction in most rural areas at that time, I would give the main credit to my often juvenile and even illiterate, but "Boswellian" *How to Teach School,* which held a firsthand record of the successes and failures of my many teachers. From its pages I gained such guiding principles as these:

A good teacher *guides* her pupils but *does not* drive them.

She encourages them to learn and to think for themselves and practices what she preaches by continuing, herself, to learn, for "gladly sholde she lerne and gladly teche."

She can succeed only if she has a genuine interest in and love for those she teaches.

She must remember to respect her pupils as individuals and to reward their efforts with praise.

She must know what she wants to do when she goes before her class and why she wants to do it.

And she must keep them interested and busy.

"Confucius says" was a popular preface to many flippant wisecracks a few years ago; but one of his truly wise observations that teachers would do well to observe is, "A good singer makes others follow his tune, and a good educator makes others follow his ideal." I was, to be sure, short on "book larnin' " when I went out to teach in Rosebud School, but I was long on ideals. An even wiser observation of the great Chinese sage, who, after a youth of poverty, established a school for "enquiring spirits who wished to be instructed in the principles of right conduct and government," was: "When the teacher is respected, then people respect what he teaches; and when people respect what he teaches, then they respect scholarship." To gain the respect of their elders, I knew I must first have the respect of my pupils. That I had had almost no discipline problems and that my pupils seemed anxious to learn were evidences that I was, in a measure, succeeding in this respect. Teaching school was wonderful fun!

Not all my time was devoted to my work, for there was much social activity among the young people of Rosebud. In addition to dances held each week in the schoolhouse and attended by young and old, there were play-parties in the homes, where we played such games as "Skip to My Lou," "Snap-out," "Weevily Wheat," "Pleased or Displeased," and "Forfeits." There were candy pullings and hayrides; and there were "singings" on Sunday night at the little country church, where Sunday School met each Sunday afternoon and an itinerant preacher conducted services the fourth Sunday in every month. There were picnics to pick up pecans, or "just because"; there were horseback rides over the countryside — and there was at least one famous snipe hunt.

At the first gathering of the young people after I came to Rosebud School, the idea of taking me on a snipe hunt had developed. I did not exactly tell them I had already participated in several successful such hunts. Thinking, in

53

fact, that it would be fun to play along with them in their fun and perhaps cook up a new angle to the hunt, I almost overdid my enthusiasm.

Before many days had passed, the night for the hunt was set; and often I saw some of my pupils who were in on the plans, looking at me over their books and giggling among themselves. One little girl who loved me too much to sit by and see me make a fool of myself tried to warn me, but I sidestepped her efforts; and when the big night came, I was ready and waiting for the hunters when they came for me.

When we reached a gully which ran through the decaying corn stubble, a heated argument ensued as to who should have the privilege of holding the sack into which the snipes would be driven. Finally, when it was decided that the honor should be given to the new teacher, I modestly accepted. Taking the only headlight, they left me to hold a big tow sack while they went off to round up the birds and drive them down the gully and into the open sack.

"When you hear us coming," they cautioned, "open the sack wide and hold it tight. Snipes are foxy, you know."

One gallant, declaring that he hated to leave me alone in the pitch dark, for they had chosen a moonless and almost starless night, offered to stay with me; but loud was the party's refusal to let him share my honor.

"This sack will be full of snipes when the hunt is finished," I boasted, as I got set for the coup.

As soon as I could hear them at a safe distance, beating the corn stubble to round up the imaginary birds, I laid down the sack, slipped noiselessly down the gully until I was out of their hearing (like a cat, I can see in the dark) and made a bee line for the lights of home. Had these been extinguished, I would have run toward the evening star, which, I had observed, hung just above the house. Slipping noiselessly into my room, I took a blanket and crawled

54

under the bed, where, in spite of my determination not to do so, I fell asleep almost at once.

When the hunters returned to the gully and found the abandoned sack, the laugh they were ready to enjoy turned first into worry and later, when no answer came to their calls, into stark panic. Scattering out over the cornfield, they searched and shouted frantically for me. At last they came to the house, woke the family, who had already blown out the lights and gone to sleep, and asked them to see if I were in my room. When Elsie found my bed apparently undisturbed, the whole group was thrown into complete Pandemonium, while I lay under the bed fast asleep.

The ringing of the telephone as Ed tried to wake "central" so they could summon the sheriff with his blood-hounds to search for me finally penetrated my deep sleep, and I crawled out and walked into the dining room, where the whole party was talking at the same time. I had won that round hands down!

Their round came a few weeks later when they took me on a coon hunt on Thursday night. They would get me home early, they had promised, when I demurred because this was a school night — and how they did keep that promise!

On a wagon made comfortable with hay we sang our way down to a thickly wooded area some distance from where I boarded. When what I felt was the proper time to go home had come and I insisted that we go, the leader of the group — a renowned coon hunter — drawled in his lazy voice:

"We'll take you home if you'll show us the way. I declare to goodness I'm plumb lost."

Insisting that anybody could find the wagon, I took the headlight from the hunter, perched it on my head and started out through the woods. Followed by the entire group, I finally came upon a little creek which I knew was in the opposite direction from home.

Back we turned and again struggled through the under-brush and briers that lay in our paths. When I reluctantly admitted that I too was lost, they built a fire, for a beacon they said; and ever so often for the remainder of the night one or two of the boys would make a determined search for the wagon. That this search was not too extensive was evident when daylight came, and the wagon was disclosed not many steps away. Why I had failed to hear some sound from the horse still puzzles me.

As Mrs. Teller was in on the plans, my worry about her alarm was wasted. It was Ed's and Elsie's presence in the hunting party and their apparent distress over our plight, in fact, that had allayed any suspicion I might have entertained.

When we reached the house, I just bathed, dressed, wolfed down an enormous breakfast, and somnolently trudged down the now trebly dusty lane to struggle through an endless day at school. They had collected their snipe-hunting debt in full!

7

After I danced "Home Sweet Home" to end the big Christmas Ball which followed a beautiful Christmas pageant presented by my students, and was driven to Cuero, where my family now lived so that the younger children could have better educational opportunities, I kept my proud family awake the remainder of the night telling them of my wonderful, wonderful school and my truly incomparable students.

While I was at home for the holidays, however, a serpent, in the form of a degenerate alcoholic with four outlaw sons of school age, invaded my little paradise. Excitement there had reached such proportions that Mr. Bennett made a special trip to town to urge me not to let rumors of threats made by these boys keep me from returning after the holidays. His trip was unnecessary, for, in my brother's private language, "neither hell nor high water" could keep me away then.

The family causing all the excitement had rented a farm and moved from Lost Creek Community when the boys, after having driven two teachers away the previous year, had that fall beaten a young teacher so severely that she was forced to spend some time in a hospital. As soon as they moved to Rosebud Community and heard of the "little sixteen-year-old kid" who was the teacher, they began boasting about how they would drive me away within a week. That they might fail to make good their boast never entered the minds of Mr. Jenkins's overgrown, out-law sons — Jesse, seventeen; Buck, sixteen; Tom, fifteen; and Jim, ten years old.

On the first Monday of the new year, I welcomed the Jenkins children into Rosebud School, assigned them to their first seats, enrolled them in classes, and began our regular work. It was my secret opinion that I could win them with gentleness, patience, and kindness; but they mistook my efforts for fear. At recess, though we invited them to play with us, they stood defiantly off in one corner of the school yard and eternally whittled with over-sized Barlow knives, which they were at great pains to display.

For the first week, things went along apparently as usual, but day by day the tension mounted as the boys stood or sat in the fence corner and whittled. As the days passed and the strain increased, I felt as if I were perched on a volcano that was about to blow its top.

I was particularly careful to remain on the school ground at all times when the Jenkinses were at school, coming to school almost by sunup to forestall their mis-behavior. On Tuesday of the second week, however, my little baseball fan had fallen on a piece of glass, and I had taken him into the house to clean and bind up the wound, when a Krause girl rushed in shouting, "Miss Cleo, come quick! Buck is killing Johnny!" Johnny was her husky brother, but the tales of Buck's prowess had overcome her — and probably Johnny.

Rushing out the door, I saw Buck sitting on Johnny, beating his head mercilessly against the hard-packed baseball diamond, and telling him just what kind of "a low-down skunk" he was. But what really froze me in my tracks was the sight of Jesse, standing between the combatants and any would-be helpers, swinging a baseball bat, and urging Buck to kill his "mangy" victim. The language he used to accompany his advice would curl the hair of a seasoned doughboy and make a hard-boiled Marine sergeant shed frustrated, envious tears.

For only an instant that seemed like a long lifetime, I stood powerless to move. Then knowing this was no time to try the power of reason, I dashed to the storage closet, picked up the rawhide buggy whip with which Henry, my superstitious ex-boyfriend, had earlier provided me half in fun, and went out, sure that this was one battle I had to win.

Since Jesse was a year older than I and considerably larger, and since my safety and job depended on the result of the fracas, I did not hesitate to use any means to subdue these outlaws. When Jesse, ignoring my command to lay down the bat, started toward me instead, I hit him across his shoulder and right arm with all the strength I had accumulated through the swing of a cotton hoe and a baseball bat.

Struck by the intense pain and just as intense surprise, he dropped the bat; and when he stooped to try to regain it, I struck him again and again with the keen whip.

Leaving the bat, he tried to close in on me, but as I backed away, I continued to apply the licks — and I was not at all particular where I applied them. Before he gave up, I had almost "cut him to ribbons," as the boastful community later reported.

The whole affair might have ended differently, had not Joe, my loyal Mexican boy, come to my defense when Tom, the fifteen-year-old Jenkins, opened his Barlow and started slipping up behind me.

The first warning I had, came when I heard in Joe's broken English, "You heet Miss Cleo, me keela you!" and saw the flash of a bigger knife than any the Jenkins gang owned. Grateful because I had let Joe come to school and had treated him just like all the other boys, Joe's father had given him the knife and told him to use it if I needed help.

Jesse, bloody and conquered, at last stood in abject submission as his body shook with convulsive sobs. Turning from him, I used the whip, again with force, on the belligerent Tom. Though Johnnie, with the aid of some other boys who had gone to his assistance as soon as Jesse's bat was immobilized, had worked Buck over rather thoroughly, I gave him a few hard licks with my whip too, just to remind him who was in control in Rosebud School.

I received my only wound in the fracas when I was too chicken-hearted to use the whip on Jim, the fourth brother — a tiny ten-year-old — who was strutting around like a bantam rooster in search of a fight. Flourishing his open Barlow and proclaiming with hair-raising profanity what his father would do about all this, he had to be punished — but not with that cruel whip, I thought. I started, therefore, to take him across my trembling knees and spank him, when, like a mad cat, he grabbed me with his sharp, dirty claws and gouged three holes in my left arm.

At last the battle was ended, having lasted from morning recess until noon. A fat, stolid little Krause girl, ignoring the brawl and sitting on the school step blissfully chewing on her thick slice of light bread spread with lard and her garlic-pungent sausage, reminded me of the hour and furnished me, as well as most of the students, with an excuse for almost hysterical laughter.

The completely crushed aggressors wanted to go home, but I had other plans for them. Taking them out to the cistern, I had them remove their ragged, bloody shirts, roll up their pants, and bathe themselves thoroughly. I furnished the soap and the rags and directed the procedure. I was fortunate they did not develop pneumonia, for it was a cool winter day.

Then I did something I had wanted to do since the day they entered school — I took a pair of scissors and cut off their tangled mops of hair. Next, I applied salve to their welts and cuts and offered them a chance to eat their lunches, but neither they nor I were hungry.

After a short interval to regain control of my shaking body, I rang the bell, and the afternoon classes were held as usual. I was a sad, weary, discouraged teacher, for I had been forced to beat, not one child, but three — an act I was then and am still rabidly opposed to.

Before I let the boys go home that afternoon, I had a long talk with them and told them I hoped they would come on to school, forget what had passed (as I would do) and be like the other boys at school. I had made the mistake, I suppose, of not using the whip on Jim too, for he had rushed home ahead of the older boys to tell how I had beaten them with a buggy whip — for no reason at all.

☆　☆　☆

Instead of going to my boarding place when I closed and locked the school, I went up to tell Mr. Bennett what I had done.

"Go on home and take care of that arm," he counseled me. "I'll take over from here."

True to his promise, the next morning he was sitting, with a shotgun across his knees, on the front steps at school when I arrived. Ed, my faithful watchdog, who left home for a while as soon as he heard my story after supper for a conference with Mr. Bennett and Mr. Krause, I learned later, had insisted that I let him drive me to school the next day, and I had gratefully accepted his offer. Mr. Krause arrived a few minutes after Ed and I made our appearance and announced that he had come to see about our supply of wood. A few minutes later Joe and Peter came riding up, each mounted behind his father. Peter's father explained that they thought we might need some wood. And they hung around as though counting every chip in the woodpile.

A few minutes before nine, Mr. Jenkins, mounted on an old swaybacked dun mare and followed by his four sons on foot, emerged from a heavy growth of post oaks through which the road ran to their house. Ominously he rode up to the school yard gate. Mr. Bennett and Ed, whose back pocket bulged suspiciously under his denim jacket, met the half-drunk, thoroughly riled visitor before he could open the gate.

When Jenkins saw the "reception committee" waiting for him, all his bluster suddenly departed, and he would have turned his horse to go home. Mr. Bennett, however, had other ideas. Wishing completely to destroy Jenkins's reputation as a "badman," he pulled the already deflated avenger from his horse and proceeded to give him a thorough beating. That was the first and the last time a trustee or anyone else ever had to defend me physically.

The four boys stayed at school that day and rarely missed a day during the remainder of the two years I taught Rosebud School. The fifteen-year-old Tom became one of my best pupils and one of my warmest friends. Jesse was one of those dull ones, now classified as "slow learners," but he did behave and he liked to play baseball. Buck, a year younger than he, though a star on the playground, was too restless to do much studying. He was the champion in arithmetic matches, however. Tom, exposed to kindness and encouragement, blossomed like a desert flower after

61

rain. And Jim became a loveable little bad boy with no special yen for books.

To be sure my salary was small, but rewards were great as my little brood worked and learned and played together while my weapon of defense sat unneeded in the closet with the broom and the dust rags. Though I was to take my weapon of defense with me when later I attacked a seemingly impossible situation at Lost Creek School, I was never forced to resort to its use again.

8

My first year at Rosebud flew by. Even Mr. Parker, after the Jenkins episode, became my best press agent, in spite of a *faux pas* I committed when he and his wife, dressed in their Sunday best, made the long drive into town the Saturday after the "Battle of the Buggy Whip," to see about my arm, which had become painfully infected, and to congratulate my parents for bringing up "such a courageous, brilliant daughter."

In spite of my crippled arm, which the doctor had treated and placed in a sling, I had put on a pair of my brother's trousers and was rushing to the stable to ride Red Bird, our imperious red stallion, the twelve miles out to our farm, while Papa followed in the buggy.

I was upstairs; I was in a hurry; the staircase was waiting; so, as I had often done before, even when dressed in my green dream-dress, I took the quickest way. Just as my ride down the banister got under way, Mr. and Mrs. Parker appeared at the front door, and I landed right in front of them. Nonchalantly, as though I were clad like a lady and had made a conventional descent of the stairs, I invited them in, turned them over to Mama and Papa, and took off on Red Bird. They never guessed that I was as much embarrassed as they were shocked.

☆   ☆   ☆

Thinking back over the year's work as I lay awake, on the night of the big picnic that would bring my first school year to a close, I thought of the precepts I had so carefully compiled in my *How To* book and felt that, in the main, I had been able to live up to most of them.

I had "ben gud to al my pupls" and had loved them — even when they were bad.

I had kept them busy, had tried to know what I expected from them and why, had almost succeeded in controlling my fiery temper, and had been forced only once to use extreme measures to control a situation.

I had read to my romance-hungry pupils, as Mr. Young had once read to me; and I had been sure that they were greeted each morning with "some bit of truth and beauty" that might "serve a turn in their lives."

Yes, I had had my good days and my bad days, my successful days and my failures, but my zest for teaching school had not diminished. Instead I was more convinced than ever that I had made the right choice of the stuff of which my Dream was made.

9

Not having enough money to go to school without borrowing it (I had been taught to run my affairs on a pay-as-you-go basis), I went to work in pleasant surroundings, for better pay than I had received for teaching and for much shorter hours. But chalk dust was in my blood; so when September came, and with it time for Institute, I left the easy job with good pay and went joyously back to take up my Dream again, this time at a salary of fifty-five dollars a month.

It was at my second Institute that I again made a fool of

myself, this time with an impromptu speech on methods of teaching agriculture. The county superintendent, a stern, straitlaced former president of a now defunct little college at Concrete, was a boyhood friend of Papa's. Hence he had watched my work and had guided me with more than professional interest. I had consequently always tried to practice my very best behavior in his presence. But on the last day of Institute, while we waited for some tardy "Eminent Speaker" to address us on "Methods of Teaching Agriculture in the Rural School," some of us younger teachers formed the nucleus of a hilarious group — too hilarious, I am sure.

To remind me of my lost dignity and, I suspect, to put me in my place, the superintendent announced that he was turning the meeting over to Miss Winslett (that was I), as he felt sure I had some good ideas about the subject. Engrossed in our fun, I did not hear what he said until I was enveloped in the blanket of silence that fell on the room and felt the eyes of all the older, more circumspect teachers, boring into my very soul.

Utter consternation gripped me when he repeated his announcement. I protested in a sickly voice, "Mr. Coffin, I can't talk before this group. They all know more than I do."

Upon his firm and somewhat testy insistence, almost paralyzed with fright, I tottered to the front of the room and looked to him for mercy. His gloating look over my discomfort and his adamant "We're waiting, Miss Winslett," summoned anger to recompense for my ignorance. I spent the next ten or fifteen minutes telling him and the group how ignorant they really were about agriculture. My experience as a cotton picker was then beginning to be the skeleton in my closet, for I remembered that select society looked down its nose at women who did manual labor. Throwing all caution to the winds, however, I painted a sad picture of life on the farm. In my effort to

64

find something to say, I even quoted "Cotton How I Hate You!" — my masterpiece.

"People who don't even know the need of agriculture can't teach the subject — and they can't tell others how to to teach it!" I added as a subtle slap at the city-bred Mr. Coffin, who knew very little of farm life and its problems.

When I made this bold statement, my harangue — and misery — were ended by a burst of applause from a hitherto unnoticed man sitting at the back of the room. Our tardy speaker had arrived, but he had come too late to save me from the bitter knowledge that I had nothing to say and had said it.

Now convinced that I would never escape the warping influence of soul-destroying cotton, I gladly went back to Rosebud, where the necessity for labor by all the family was accepted as a natural law. Only a few days after school began, in fact, I went out for another bout with my old enemy and its torturous prickly bolls. A young wife whose husband had been committed to a mental institution lived on a small farm in the Guadalupe River Valley, and did most of the farm work herself, for her three small children were too young to work.

When a huge rise was on its way down the river, and her field was white with ungathered cotton, school was closed for the day, and every able-bodied person in the neighborhood turned out to help gather the cotton before the flood waters came. Nobody expected me to help, for teachers then were truly something very special, and I had kept my cotton-picking experience a carefully guarded secret. But I put on my oldest clothes, borrowed one of Mrs. Teller's "split" bonnets, and went with Ed and Elsie to help with the work — an act which added to, rather than detracted from, the esteem I enjoyed in the community. These people would have scorned the idea that Southern gentlewomen did not do field work.

10

Now the end of my second year had come, bringing to a close a chapter in my life that beggars words to express the joys and satisfactions I had experienced. It marked the close of my little-girl impetuosities and my unbounded idealism. But my Dream remained as bright as ever.

Two of my pupils had married, and I had "stood up" with both of them — later one of these named her little daughter for me. My tobacco-chewing, would-be-boyfriend-pupil had married a "cotton mill girl" in town and had gone to work there.

I had visited in the home of every pupil I taught and had spent the night in most homes — even in the Jenkinses' pitifully bare shack when the father was away from home on a trip. I had enjoyed tamales made from a freshly butchered hog one afternoon in Peter's neat flower-enhanced home and had drunk coffee and eaten delicious *pan de dulce* at Joe's home while the boys sat proudly by me, their mothers hovered anxiously over me, and bashful little beady-eyed boys and girls peeped around the doors or through the windows.

I had nursed the sick, and had grieved and worked with Elsie and Ed to try to alleviate the suffering of their mother, who was dying of cancer and did not know it. I had seen my students meet and defeat selected speakers, essayists, and spellers from Cuero's schools, and had been invited to tell a spring meeting of teachers why teaching school is fun. I was an experienced teacher.

But now the end of my second year had come — and

with it, a grave decision. I could sign the new contract that Rosebud's trustees had already drawn up for me and return in the fall to a community which I loved and in which I knew I was loved — or I could accept an offer to teach in Cuero's grade school, where the work would be much lighter — or I could risk my reputation by accepting the unusual offer of the job at Lost Creek School, where no teacher had finished a whole school term for a period extending over more than five years.

If I chose the latter, my salary from the state would be the maximum for rural teachers — sixty-five dollars per month. This would be supplemented by two large landholders who, desiring to stop the migration of their best tenants to farms where better schools were available, would pay me thirty-five dollars each month from their own pockets. One hundred dollars per month was indeed a stupendous salary, but I still think the factor that really influenced my decision most was the challenge the problems offered at Lost Creek.

Whatever the inciting factor was is not really important, for against the advice of my family and most of my friends, but encouraged and supported by Mr. Coffin, the bedeviled superintendent to whom the situation at Lost Creek was an ever-present worry, I signed the contract to teach Lost Creek School the next year.

PART THREE

Be the Labor Great or Small

1

The summer following my decision to leave Rosebud and go to Lost Creek was not spent in idleness. I went to school twelve weeks in San Antonio. It was here that I cashed in on my skill in dancing, by acting as the "talented young lady instructor" in Professor Penbroke's School of Dancing for Young Ladies and Gentlemen.

My academic accomplishments suffered that summer, I am sure, for my enthusiasm for and interest in my Terpsichorean activities overshadowed any interest such previously fascinating subjects as history and science could offer. That this loss of enthusiasm was partly due to my delight in dancing and the consequent long hours I spent at the studio I readily admit, but that it was also due to the mediocrity of my teachers I firmly believe.

One teacher I still remember with extreme distaste. Clad in an ill-fitting, more than slightly soiled, sleazy gray dress, she sat before our class day after day and combed her scanty, dandruff-infested hair with an amazingly dirty, broken-tooth comb while she expounded on the bad manners, poor taste, ignorance, and extreme stupidity of the young people in her classes. Rejecting her, I also rejected all interest in the subject she was supposed to teach, though history, next to English, had been my favorite subject.

When the twelve weeks of summer school ended, I, for the first time in all my school experience, gladly shook the dust of knowledge from my feet, just as sadly parted

71

with the glamorous stardust of dancing school, and went somewhat reluctantly back home to prepare for my greatest test as a teacher.

I had been at home only a few days when I packed a small bag, which Papa tied to the pommel of my saddle, mounted Chico, our favorite saddle horse, and rode out to Lost Creek School about twenty miles from home to look over the situation. I believed then, and believe even more strongly now, that when a fellow is faced with a fight, he should strike the first blow — if possible.

Having written to one of the two large landholders, a Mr. Allan, about my desire to visit Lost Creek to survey its needs and make advance plans for the year, I received a brief note from his wife, inviting me to stay with them while I was in the community. With her note came a warning from Mr. Allan that I would not be released from my contract if what I found at the school should discourage me. When I read his letter, I began to realize that things must be really bad at Lost Creek School.

Though I thought I was prepared for the worst, the sight that greeted me when I rode up to the school at Lost Creek late one hot August afternoon would have brought despair to a person with more courage than I possessed, for a nightmare of neglect and utter desolation met my eyes.

I tied my horse to a rotted post, from which a broken gate hung drunkenly by one rusty hinge; and, with my heart in my boots and a terrible vacuum where my stomach normally lay, I forced my steps through the waist-high Johnson grass and cockleburs to the decaying steps of the derelict that was Lost Creek School.

Nearly every pane was broken from its gaping windows, and what had apparently been muddy gray paint applied in some distant, more affluent day curled from the warped boards between whose cracks I knew the cold winds would whistle in a few weeks. The most depressing picture, however, awaited me inside the building, which I entered with no difficulty, for the door swung wide open, its shattered lock attesting to some visitor's contempt for restraint of his personal liberty.

Inside, chaos, dirt, and destruction held absolute sway. Desks, many torn from the floor, were buried under a shroud of dust; and the floor was littered with broken glass, paper, insects, and spitballs. Dirt-daubers had attached their mud houses to the uncovered rafters and dingy walls, but more repulsive than the dauber nests was the almost complete blanket of spitballs that covered walls, furniture, blackboards, and especially the teacher's desk.

Quite at home with the spitballs on the board were suggestive pictures drawn by some lewd artist who, not trusting his skill to express his ideas with chalk, had added obscene, crudely spelled, but unmistakable explanations of his art. I guessed that his was the hand that shattered the lock on the door.

Feeling that one more minute in these surroundings would result in tears of despair or cowardly retreat, I hurried back through the high grass and weeds and rode on to the Allan home, while over and over, in my shocked mind I cried, "Why, O why did I ever agree to come to this godforsaken place?"

Mr. Coffin, in his anxiety to get another victim for the troublesome post had apparently evaded the truth when he assured me, "It's just about like most of our country schools. It's fairly comfortable and it has a big playground."

I was an extremely quiet, appetiteless guest at the Allan table that night. "What can I do? Where shall I begin? How can I teach in such a dump?" so filled my mind that I had difficulty listening to the eternal monologue the master of the house began when I arrived and was still continuing when I rode away two days later.

When I interrupted the continuous tale of his woes as the result of a long line of sorry teachers in Lost Creek, to suggest that maybe the unfavorable conditions under which the teacher and her pupils had to work had contributed to their failure, he scoffed at the idea.

"They don't need no better," he almost shouted. (I soon learned that he did not like his opinions challenged.) "They wouldn't take keer of it if we did fix that schoolhouse up."

When the eyes of his frightened, mousy little wife looked appealingly into mine and I saw the dread in the eyes of his pimply-faced son, who had been boarded in town since he started to school "so he could get a good education," I did not press my point further.

Before I went to sleep that night, I had reached these conclusions: First, I could expect no help from Mr. Allan, but I would collect every cent of the money he had contracted to pay me. Second, I would not resign, as that afternoon I had been tempted to do. But I would not try to teach for even one day in such conditions as prevailed at Lost Creek School. That I would have Cleanup Day was my final decision before I fell into a restless, troubled sleep, in which the opinionated Mr. Allan, the drunken Mr. Jenkins, and the antiquated Mr. Parker from my Rosebud days were somehow involved.

When I broached my idea of a cleanup day to Mr. Allan the next morning, he opposed it on the grounds that everybody was too busy picking cotton. "I'll go down with my haymower the week before school starts," he promised, "and cut down the grass and weeds. Then you and the kids can clean up the schoolhouse when school starts. We'll git the winderpanes put in before a norther comes." I did not argue with Mr. Allan about the cleanup plan, but his opposition convinced me that I must carry it through.

74

All day I spent visiting the families who would have children in school that fall. I wanted to start the day off with a visit to Mr. Lawrence, who was to pay the other half of my thirty-five-dollar bonus. But Mrs. Allan assured me she was too busy to go with me, and I knew convention would not permit my going unchaperoned, since he was a personable, not-too-old bachelor, living alone in his imposing two-story white house on a high hill overlooking acres and acres of cotton.

My opportunity to talk to him came that afternoon, however, when he "dropped by" the home of one of his tenants shortly after I had arrived. I found him truly interested in anything that might help solve the Lost Creek problems, which made it so difficult to keep good tenants on his farms. He immediately approved the idea of Cleanup Day, agreeing to publicize its date himself and to help with the work when the day came. We agreed that Thursday before school was to open on the following Monday should be the day for our undertaking.

The day after my talk with Mr. Lawrence I rode back home, "a sadder and a wiser" girl. I think I really grew up on that three-day visit.

2

The week following my visit to Lost Creek, I attended my third Institute; but I was no longer the gay, mischievous, carefree girl I had been in previous years. The blight of Lost Creek had already placed its stamp on me, or so I was seriously warned by one of my fun-loving cohorts of former Institutes. And what she said was true, for I was wondering if I had not "bit off more than I could chew."

Though the horrifying picture of Lost Creek School as I had seen it that memorable afternoon was partly responsible for my new seriousness, it was not wholly to blame. I had again come into contact with the malevolent influence of my old enemy, and had been struck as never before with the results of Cotton's degradation and destruction of human beings.

Wives of Mr. Allan's tenants, existing in hovels worse than his pigpens, had stared at me stolidly and suspiciously as with their greasy aprons they wiped the dust from a chair for me. In answer to my questions about their school, each had made almost the identical reply:

"It jist seems like don't nobody keer about school. The kids is mean, and the teachers is skeerd of 'em. If I was you, I wouldn't fool with 'em."

Though some of the farmers were in better circumstances, those on the Lawrence and Kimcek farms particularly, the entire community showed the soul-destroying effect of the plant that can "promise more, give less, disappoint the deepest, and fail from more causes than any other wayward plant that grows."

As I reflect on it now, it seems impossible that such conditions existed not so many years ago in an area in Texas now dotted with neat, comfortable, electric-lighted, radio- and television-entertained homes. From these homes boys and girls are picked up daily by fast buses and transported over paved roads to ultramodern schools in town, where they are the peers of the no-longer more-privileged city students.

It is true that I still listened with rapt attention to the good lectures at Institute that fall and took notes too. But I rejected completely the talks of those who, like me the previous year, had nothing to say and said it. Vainly all week I waited for Mr. Coffin or some high-powered speaker invited in to tell us how to teach, to suggest a solution for such problems as existed at Lost Creek. I still reveled in the formal banquet, the watermelon party — this time with no spelling match to tie me in knots — the silent-movie party, followed by an ice cream supper in the park by the firehouse and the crowning event — the Reception and Grand Ball on the last night.

But, in spite of all my previous dramatization of hardships inflicted on me through my farm experiences, I had, for the first time, met something at Lost Creek so tragic that it was overwhelming. How I could combat the blight which Cotton had spread over Lost Creek concerned me more than how to prepare a daily schedule or how to make a drawing of a newfangled silo.

3

As the days that intervened between my return home from Institute and the date of our Cleanup Day flew by, my old idealism began gradually to return. My old enthusiasm for reform reasserted itself to such an extent that one night I heard Papa tell Mama, "She'll be all right now, she has her fighting clothes on again."

The day I was to go out to help with our Cleanup Day developed into quite a picnic. Papa came in from our little store — the family was again in town for school — bringing with him two large galvanized buckets, a broom, a mop, and several packages of Rub-No-More, a powder so strong it would peel the dirt off the walls and the skin off the hands. Mama and I prepared a bountiful lunch; so, ready to do battle with neglect, we left home by daylight for our drive out to Lost Creek.

When we arrived, we found a crew of Mexicans from Mr. Lawrence's farms busy with hoes, chopping up the tough stubble that remained after Mr. Allan — true to his promise, though refusing to participate in the official day — had mowed the grass and weeds.

Mr. Lawrence, who was there also, and Mr. Kimcek, a thrifty Polish patron who owned a small farm and a large bunch of children, were busily nailing the warped boards back on the sides of the schoolhouse and placing weather stripping over the gaping cracks. A few already tired-looking farm women and some large, gawky girls stood near the steps, waiting for someone to tell them what to do.

Papa, with the eager help of two big boys, took charge of replacing the broken windowpanes, while Mama and I went inside with the waiting women and girls to wage war on the daubers, wasps, spitballs, and accumulated dirt. When we finished, every inch of the floor, walls, and even the rafters had been scrubbed; and the new windows had been thoroughly washed inside and out.

After all the panes, paid for by Mr. Lawrence, as were the other supplies for the repairs, were in place and washed sparklingly clean, the amateur carpenters hung solid wooden shutters, which protected the windows, and fastened them inside with strong iron hooks. A strong lock was placed on the reinforced door, and though Lost Creek School late that afternoon did not resemble a palace, neither was it the eyesore it had been when the sun rose that morning.

The problem of improving the building and grounds was not the only one that faced me. There was only one place anywhere near school where I might find board and room. This was in the small, bare home of the newly-married sixteen-year-old Allan daughter and her eighteen-year-old husband. When I had had a cold fried egg between two slices of dry bread for my lunch for five consecutive days, followed each night by a supper of one can of potted meat, three slices of bread, and three glasses of separated milk (they sold the cream) for the three of us, I knew that I must seek other living quarters. None being available, unless I shared a squalid room with several children and shared a bed with at least one, I moved back to town at the end of the first week and rode horseback seven miles out to the school and back home each day.

4

On the opening day of Lost Creek School, when the victims of malevolent Cotton stood silent as I attempted to open school with the singing of "America" and stumblingly tried to join me in reading the Twenty-Third Psalm, I was struck anew with the barrenness of the lives of these people, and I determined that day that I must try to wipe the vacant looks from those tragic faces and bring something of beauty and happiness into those starved lives.

Many of the parents, having heard of or helped with cleaning up the school, had laid aside King Cotton's yoke for a short time and had come to school for the opening day, as on my visits I had urged them to do.

Before I began organizing classwork, I stood before the group and talked to them with all the eloquence I had learned "saying speeches" on the Friday afternoons of my childhood and with all the sincerity and compassion engendered by their hopeless, apathetic looks, in which I thought hopefully was a trace of rebellion against their slavelike condition.

"I do not believe in whipping," I told them — and their doubt-filled, fleeting smiles told me they had heard of the "Battle of the Buggy Whip." "Might does not make right," I continued. "Force is not necessary where fairness, kindness, and a spirit of cooperation and brotherly love prevail."

I hoped to have a school, I continued, in which we could all work together as one big congenial family. A school is not the responsibility of the teacher alone, I earnestly assured them. I looked at the boys and girls as I suggested that school would be a good place for all of us to gather for fun and fellowship as well as for work, but not a flicker of interest showed in their lackluster eyes.

When I finished, I asked the parents if they had anything to say. One of the women who had helped wash the walls of the school arose and said, "I'm ready to help you, Teacher. I'm tired of these here kids runnin' the teachers off, but I don't think you can git along with these kids without whuppin' 'em."

Mr. Kimcek said without rising, "Vell, I tink maybe ve like a little fun."

Mr. Lawrence came and, standing beside me, made an earnest appeal to all present, especially to the boys and girls, to help change Lost Creek's reputation as an outlaw school. Pledging himself to help bring about this change, he sat down. I knew I had found another Mr. Bennett, my tower of strength at Rosebud School.

From the group I was most interested in — the boys and girls themselves — came no response. With a well-here-I-am-what-are-you-going-to-do-about-it look, they sat and cracked their knuckles and shuffled their feet and waited impassively.

One boy, in his early teens I judged, took out his thinly whittled paddle and, as I prepared to enroll the group, made a "bull's-eye" with a wad of partly masticated paper on the large bell on the desk over which I leaned.

Without hesitation, while a dead, dread silence fell on the group, I walked back to the offender, led him to the desk and said in a quiet voice, "Please remove the spitball, fellow. Our schoolroom is nice and clean. Wouldn't you like to keep it that way?" and went on with my work at the desk without further notice of the crestfallen sharp-shooter. Later I learned he was the champion shot of the entire school, in which shooting spitballs at targets in the schoolroom, both animate and inanimate, had been the chief sport.

It seemed a custom in Lost Creek that on the first day of school no classwork was done. Instead, when the pre-liminaries were cared for, school was dismissed until the next day. I was not aware of this custom and so was ready to begin real classwork, when one of the waiting parents

80

hesitantly told me it was time for him and his children to go home and begin picking cotton again. Discovering that none of the pupils had brought his lunch nor had expected to spend the day at school, I dismissed them, to reassemble the next day at nine o'clock. Now my great test at Lost Creek School had begun.

5

Though my buggy whip occupied a place in the corner of the room, where, strangely, no one molested it, I was never forced to use it during the two years I worked with the people of Lost Creek. I do not mean all the children suddenly reformed — they did not — but forms of discipline other than beatings were much more effective with girls and boys whose skins had almost grown calluses in the spots where switches, belts, boards, razor straps, or even wet ropes had so often landed, both at school and at home.

One of the chief problems for many years had been the maintenance of decent outdoor privies. They seemed to be objects of great interest to some of the young perverts of the community. In an attempt to stamp out the obscenities which soon began to appear in the privies, I appealed to the entire school, talking to the boys alone and then to the girls, for the word *privy* was not used in mixed groups. But in spite of my appeals, the vulgar pictures and terms grew worse.

Finally turning detective, late one afternoon, I caught two of the older boys, who never created a disturbance during class but who also never seemed to learn anything, busily sketching particularly vile pictures on the walls of the girls' privy. Walking boldly up to the open door, I invited the artists to come with me to the schoolhouse, and surprisingly, they did.

There I bade them fill a bucket with water, to which I added more than a generous portion of Rub-No-More and two large rags. Then I marched them back to the scene of their misdeeds and suggested coldly but quietly that they clean up the place.

When they had finished there, I took them to the boys' privy, which for some strange reason was just inside the fence that bordered the public road. While they scrubbed and I kept watch, a man and his wife — the two best news-spreaders in the whole community — came by from town. Soon the story of the second cleanup day became public property.

Before I could institute any type of school or community recreation, I must, I realized, first clean up a situaton that forestalled any semblance of community cooperation and unity. Soon after school opened, I discovered that Lost Creek playground was divided into four little nations — in one area was Little Germany; in another, Little Poland and Bohemia; in a third — the rockiest and least desirable — Little Mexico; and in the fourth — the most desirable part of the grounds — Little America, as these occupants would have smugly labeled their territory. A more fitting term would have been Little Poor-White-Trash, for, in the main, this was the dirtiest, dullest, and most antagonistic of all the groups. Most of the "American" boys and girls from the more privileged homes did not attend Lost Creek School, for they boarded in town and went to a good school.

In each area some type of ball game seemed to be the chief sport, though some of the little girls in the "American" space had a playhouse under a low live oak tree, which grew by the school steps, where they played with

82

dolls made of corncobs, dishes made of broken glass and pottery, and furniture made of large flat rocks, old stumps, and short logs laboriously rolled to the playhouse.

For the first few days after school began, I spent all recess periods and the noon hours visiting the little republics. For my first visit to Little Mexico, I chose a noon period. Taking my lunch, no longer a cold fried-egg sandwich, I strolled down to the rocky area that bordered a deeply eroded gully and sat down with the suddenly tongue-tied group, ready to eat.

At once all the members of the amazed group arose with their tin pails clutched in their hands and stood at servile attention. I finally prevailed upon them to sit down again, but they sat with their eyes trained on me while I struggled to swallow the food I had so pleasantly anticipated. Staring and silent they sat, looking like stray curs accustomed to nothing but abuse.

As I arose to go to the pump for a drink, they arose in a body and stood silent until I reached the pump. Then a bedlam of excited words in their native tongue burst forth from Little Mexico as its people discussed the unheard-of act of a teacher's sitting down to eat with a group of what that community called Greasers, or Pepper Bellies.

The excitement was not restricted to this one area, however. It came from all directions, but loudest from Little America. One of the boys — the larger of my outdoor scrubbing team, in fact — came up to remonstrate with me.

"White folks jist don't eat with Mescans, Teacher. You'll be hearin' about this." And it seemed to me he licked his chops in anticipation.

As I went from group to group and saw the pitiful makeshift equipment with which these children played, I began to understand the reason for their abuse of the schoolhouse. Since rocks were the most plentiful playground equipment and windows made good targets, the result was inevitable. Too, because the teachers here could spend little time with any one pupil, and almost never had any provision for challenging seatwork for the unoccupied students, naturally spitball contests furnished them outlets for their restless, unsatisfied spirits and idle hands.

6

I had much time to think as I rode to and from school each day, and slowly an idea was evolving in my mind.

One Friday morning as a part of our opening exercise, I read "Aladdin's Lamp" to the no longer impassive group. Then I asked them to think carefully what they would wish for if they could have the magic lamp for a few minutes and could wish for playground equipment.

Hands began to wave from all parts of the room. "So that all of you can tell me," I explained, "I'll let you write what your wish would be."

Those who could write fell to work at once. Those who had not yet learned to write came to my desk and whispered their wishes, and these I recorded on a sheet of paper. When they had finished, I stacked all the wishes together to read that night at home. So great was my curiosity, however, that, as soon as four o'clock came and my "housekeeping crew" had swept the floors and made the building ready for the next day, I sat down to study the wishes.

That the greatest number of wishes were for balls and bats and baseball gloves did not surprise me. Often I had seen many a disappointing conclusion to a game, when the baseball, made of threads raveled from a discarded sock, painstakingly wrapped round and round a small rock and covered with a piece of the best duck from a worn-out cotton sack, ceased to be. Some potential Babe Ruth, taking a mighty swing with the wide board whittled at one end to fit his hands, would literally knock the cover off the ball. As what should have been a home run unraveled into a long string with a rock at its end, the frustration of the batter was too tragic to observe. No wonder they spent their wishes on real balls.

The little girls who played with the corncob dolls wanted real dolls, and most of them specified "bisket" dolls with real gold-colored hair and blue eyes that would open and shut. Several wished for real tea sets, and one ventured a wish for a little doll cradle. Marbles ranked high on the list; and, what pleased me most, nearly all of them asked for books — "pitcher" books, poetry books, books like the one from which I had just read about the magic lamp.

One little boy had written, "They ain't no use in playin' this wishin' game they ain't no Sandy Claws."

At home that night when my persistent Mohawk Club member came, bringing a gaily beribboned box of "King's Chocolates — Fit for American Queens," I suggested that instead of our usual trip to the movies, we plan how to take "Sandy Claws" out to Lost Creek in late October. All my family gathered in the conference, the result of which was a busy weekend for all of us.

The next morning Mama set to work making the necessary equipment for a doll cradle, whose measurements had been furnished by Gus, the important Mohawker, who was employed in a downtown lumberyard; and I went to town to see about balls, bats, books, and dolls.

The owner of the hardware-variety store, learning the purpose of my purchases made a gift of the entire lot; so all the money I could afford for the project was then left for books. Since there was no bookstore in town and the books had to be ordered, I was forced to be content, for the present, with magazines bought from the newsstand. To these were added a supply of construction paper, scissors, wax crayons, paste, and water colors.

On my way home I dropped by the lumberyard to see how the cradle plans were progressing and found Mr. Waddell, the manager, Gus the bookkeeper, and one of my favorite dancing partners busy at work. They were not only making the cradle but were also building two sturdy, small tables and benches to be used by the little homemakers for their tea parties.

Anxious to have the surprise all ready before Monday, Gus, my little eight-year-old brother Matt, and I went out to Lost Creek on Sunday afternoon. While Gus and Matt measured and laid off a baseball diamond in the smoothest part of the large school ground and pegged down the canvas-covered bases Gus had also made, I set up the little girls' wishes inside the building. At the front of the room I placed two golden-haired "bisket" dolls, two china dolls outgrown by my sisters and dressed in new clothes by Mama, and the cradle and tables and benches. Marbles and tea sets were ready for little hands, and the bright magazines were laid about the room on the desks. That we would soon have some bookshelves and a cabinet for our materials was determined that day, for Gus, seeing the need, promised to have one ready for us within that week.

I kept the door closed on Monday morning until time for school to begin. When the door was opened and the pupils came in, their looks of amazement, unbelief, then unrestrained happiness sent me out the back door to hide my tears — my first since coming to Lost Creek.

The day of the early visit of "Sandy Claws" marked a change in the boys and girls of Lost Creek. I had that day explained that the bats, balls, and gloves belonged as much to Juan Espinoza as they did to Roger Mills or Peter Kimcek or Adolph Wagner, and that the dolls and other toys were as much the property of Esperanza Jasso as of Lola Jacobs, or Marta Kimcek or Hulda Wagner. If they did not want to play together, I explained, that was their privilege, but those who did play together would use the toys.

Thus a very successful miniature American melting pot began, though I did have some "conferences," not always placid, with some of the mamas and papas in the community.

As reports of the newly furnished playhouse under the oak tree and of the baseball games played with real balls and bats spread over the countryside, it was a rare day that we did not have visitors who came to see what was happening at Lost Creek School.

Paul Lawrence, always spick-and-span, was the most frequent visitor, tying his big roan at the school yard gate, and catching a few "flys" or admiring the work of the busy little homemakers. Often he found it necessary to ride part of the way home with Teacher — on his way to see about one of his more distant farms over on the river — and talk over the needs of his community.

On one of his visits one day, he commented on the still unfilled bookshelves that Gus had made for our school; and before the day ended, he had brought a veritable treasure trove from his own library. Until that day, though I knew his fields and pastures were vast, I had not realized he was the owner of such riches. Books were then, as they still are, to me, truly great riches.

In what seemed like a few days, Christmas came. We had worked up a simple program, which, because of a freezing rain and the stage fright of the few who in order to perform had dared the winter storm, was limited in both performers and audience. But the enjoyment and pride of the few who did come sent me home, not as troubled as I had been in September, but still not content that the lives of the people in Lost Creek should be so empty.

7

Enjoying a round of holiday dances, parties, dinners, and dates (all holidays were big events in the lives of the Winslett clan), I put aside the worries about my teaching.

But as the season neared its close, I grew eager to go back to my children and my work.

The morning I rode back out to start the new year, a "blue whistler" was blowing straight in my face so that Chico and I were forced to slow our pace. Freezing to the bone already, I dreaded the cold building that would greet me, and the ensuing cold day in a room that resisted all efforts to heat, since most of the heat was lost among the exposed rafters. As I topped the hill and looked down on my little school, I saw smoke billowing from the chimney and said a little prayer of thanks for some thoughtful early riser.

Unsaddling Chico and turning him loose in a small thicket of trees, where a rick of hay awaited him, I hastened into the comfort of a surprisingly warm room. I could not believe what I saw. The rough rafters had been covered with a ceiling, painted a very light gray. This explained the unusual warmth. But it was not the greatest miracle, for placed against the side wall near my desk was an organ, a replica of the one we had at home.

Searching for the answer to all this, I found written on the board: "Happy New Year, Teacher. The boys and I brought 'Sandy Claws' to you. The organ was my mother's. Play it for the kids — Paul. P.S. Let's start a Sunday School — P.L.L."

As I sank into my chair, overcome with surprise and gratitude, I recalled how I had tried unsuccessfully to stop Matt from boasting to Paul about my organ-playing. "She can play this old piano good, too," he bragged (he was my greatest fan and most devoted slave), "but the organ music is prettier." And Paul, who had dropped by home on Sunday afternoon — to see if we needed anything out at school, he explained — had decided to place the organ in school for the children to enjoy.

I had come out quite early to place assignments, a Bible reading, and "memory gems" on the board; hence some time elapsed before the boys and girls, stolid and unresponsive only four months before, came rushing into the warm

88

schoolhouse, all talking and laughing at the same time. They had met out in the cold down at the far end of the school yard and had come in a group to see what Teacher thought of her surprise, for news of Paul's gift had spread through the community.

Oblivious of their painful, almost frozen, blue hands and their chilled bodies, they crowded around the organ, instead of the warm stove, for the organ, a marvel of elegance, was the first some of them had ever seen. They could hardly wait to hear its tones, all urging, "Please play it, Teacher!"

Longing to express the gratitude and humility I felt, and wishing to play for this first number something that would have lasting worth, slowly I ran my fingers over the keys. Then swelling from the organ came "Praise God from Whom All Blessings Flow." And with the music I sang the words all alone to that enthralled group. What I lacked in ability to play or to sing, I made up in sincerity and depth of feeling.

When I yielded to their pleas of "Sing it again," a strong baritone voice joined me. Looking toward the door, I saw Paul, standing with unashamed tears in his eyes as he sang.

"America," "Red River Valley," and "Red Wing" — all requested numbers in which the group joined — and "Auld Lang Syne," sung by Paul and me because we were starting a new year, made up our initial concert. Though I insisted we must now get down to real business, Paul remained, apparently as interested in the arithmetic lesson which followed as he had been in the music.

His presence, however, flustered me more than the presence of the three trustees on my first day at Rosebud when I was a rank beginner. I therefore laughingly but firmly sent him home so my students could keep their minds on their work.

Paul's New Year's Greeting, with its postcript still on the board, started the next reform at Lost Creek. "Let's do have a Sunday School," begged Hulda, who had read Paul's "P.S." And the others took up the plea.

I knew that I was treading dangerous ground in a community where Lutherans, Roman Catholics, Baptists, "Campbellites," and "Holy Rollers" carried on incessant religious warfare though no sort of religious services were held there except an occasional "protracted" meeting held in the summer under a crude arbor. I suggested, therefore, that they go home and talk it over with their parents. Then if enough people were interested, we would meet the next Sunday and organize. This would mean another trip back out here for me, but that this was beyond the call of duty did not occur to me. The Lost Creek people were my people, and to serve them was my duty.

Response favoring the Sunday School was surprising, the only serious opposition coming from Mr. Allan, who thought such a plan would lead to trouble, and from Mr. Grimsby, a devout "Holy Roller," who was likely at any moment to take off through the brush shouting in "The Unknown Tongue."

"I jist don't want none uh my kids learnin' nothin' but the religion that's right," he made a special trip to tell me.

Still, with so many people anxious to have the school, the news went out on Friday that a non-denominational Sunday School was to be organized at the schoolhouse Sunday afternoon at three-thirty. Thus was begun a community Sunday School which was to continue until consolidation, with its consequent buses to town, wrote *finis* to Lost Creek School.

It was during this first week after the Christmas holidays, while the community was humming with news of the organ and plans for Sunday School, that my pupils began to bring me invitations from their mamas to spend a night in their homes. I accepted every one I received, though often my visit caused children to sleep on a cold, hard

90

pallet while I slept in their bed, often not too warm itself. In a land where cotton often rotted in the fields, most of these people used corn shucks instead of cotton to stuff their mattresses.

When I was indignantly condemning that practice at home one night in the presence of my oldest brother, who was home for a visit, he remarked dryly, "Well, I'd think that wouldn't bother you. I'd expect you to choose a bed stuffed with cockleburs rather than one stuffed with cotton."

Far overshadowing the physical discomfort often suffered on these visits was the fact that in every home my visit was treated as a great honor, and I was entertained with the best that home possessed. Teacher was welcomed like visiting royalty.

8

One particularly cold morning, following a week of incessant rain, I reached school later than was my custom, for I had been forced to ride more carefully and twice had been forced to swim Chico across usually dry gullies. When I reached school the handful of boys and girls who had braved the cold and rain were huddled around the stove, which was just beginning to warm up. Over them, like a pall, hung the dreadful odor of pariah skunk. As the heat increased, so did the odor. Since often some boy came to school with traces of his successful hunt still clinging to his clothes, I was not greatly disturbed; but as I approached my desk and found the stench almost overpowering, I felt sure that a real skunk was there.

Two boys armed with baseball bats and I, with my buggy whip, went to the attack. Gingerly opening a drawer, we found a dead skunk stretched out among some papers. Though we got rid of the skunk and set the reeking drawer under the dripping eaves for a bath, it was almost impossible to stay in the room, which had to be closed

91

for warmth. The odor seemed to increase when Pablo, the only one of his nationality present, came near; but I made no effort to find the offender.

Instead, I asked Pablo — a slow learner who, because of his grimaces and gesticulations when he tried to read, often furnished sly amusement for the school — to stand by the organ and lead the group in our song session, for he loved to sing. The remainder of that day he hung around me, with a hangdog look on his vacuous face, trying to anticipate my wishes.

When, though the rain had stopped and several days had passed, neither Pablo nor his bright little sister Maria had come to school since the skunk episode, I rode over to their little shack to see why they were absent.

Their father apologetically met me at the gate and began in his inadequate English, "Pablo he no go to school no more. He loco — he got no sense — you good to Pablo. He bad boy. Me beat him mooch."

And he had beaten him "mooch." Using a rope, which he had first soaked in a horse trough, he had beaten poor Pablo unmercifully, as his bruises testified.

It seems that Pablo, troubled by his conscience, had confided his guilt to little Maria, who, shocked by his misdeed, had told her parents. Grateful for my kindness to the Mexican children in school, the father, feeling that Pablo had betrayed his people, had wreaked his anger and embarrassment on poor, stupid Pablo.

When the apologetic father learned that I was anxious for Pablo and Maria to come back to school, he caught my hand in both his and and broke into a flood of Spanish too rapid for me to follow. A few days later Maria confided in a whisper that she had a new little sister named Cleo.

Why Pablo had placed the skunk in the desk remained a mystery, for his debt was more than paid, and I have always abhorred post-mortems. I wondered, however, if I had not failed Pablo somehow, and he had used the skunk in his search for his own particular place in the sun.

9

Though I went to the courthouse at the end of every month to have Mr. Coffin approve my voucher which had already been signed by trustees Allan, Kimcek, and Lawrence, I volunteered no information about the progress of my school and extended him no invitation to visit us. I was, to be honest, still a bit put out because his information about Lost Creek had left me unprepared for the true conditions there and also because he, having encouraged me to take the place, had made no effort to see if I needed his help to solve the difficulties that confronted me there. His attitude had been, "It's your job. You handle it."

Either rumors of the goings-on at Lost Creek School or the law requiring the county superintendent to visit every school in his county at least once each year, finally had its effect, for one day about eleven o'clock, Mr. Coffin's buggy, lopsided from the weight it daily bore, and drawn by an indifferent, unhurried sorrel mare, ambled up to the school yard gate and discharged its august passenger.

Immediately the entire school became Pandemonium. One little boy, in his extreme excitement, rushed up to my desk and shouted, "Get ready, Teacher. That man can fuss like hell!"

Into the ensuing shocked silence, like a battleship ready for attack, Mr. Coffin ploughed through the front door and, glaring threateningly to his right and left, wallowed up the aisle. Taking only a brief time for greetings, I conducted him to my desk, where he overflowed my chair. Then I continued our regular classes until noon, while Mr. Coffin, at first tense and bellicose, gradually relaxed and watched us.

When I had dismissed school for lunch, and our visitor and I sat eating the food I had brought from home, I learned why he had come in prepared to do battle. On his enforced visits in previous years, every time he turned his back to the room, he had been the target for the spitball

93

sharpshooters, who, he insisted, respected neither God nor man.

Thinking of the back of his head where lay fat folds bristling with stiff, short, porcupinelike hairs, each separate hair pointing in its own particular direction, I burst into hilarious laughter, in which he, though apparently puzzled, reluctantly joined. He did not know that it had been a whispered wish for a paddle and a spitball to use on the target presented by the back of his head that had set off the hilarity at Institute the day I was forced to make the memorable speech on agriculture. It was not difficult for me to understand the temptation that the Lost Creek children could not resist.

Mr. Coffin spent the remainder of the day with us, asking in surprise, "Is it four o'clock?" when school was dismissed for the day.

We had made no effort to impress him, but had simply carried on our usual work, deviating only slightly when the students, anxious to show off their organ and their vocal ability, begged for a music period before classes after lunch. I agreed reluctantly, for I knew that what was beautiful music to them would be considered poor to one accustomed to real music. Since their happiness was more important than his opinion of my musical ability, we had had the singsong, in which he surprisingly had joined.

10

Those students who had participated in the Christmas program and those who had — because of timidity, bad weather, or parental objection — failed to participate now began to urge that we have a big closing-school program — with a real play and everything. To meet this plea, since the end of school was flying toward us, and I could not wait for new material, I was forced to build the program around material I already had.

The *piéce de resistance* was to be "Axin' Poppa's Permission," a trivial one-act play to be done in blackface with "broad" Negro dialect. It was filled with action and lines that, in those days in communities like Lost Creek, would bring down the house.

Though the names of the students who took the parts of the Negro father, the dusky mother, and the lovesick but scared Negro lover are lost in the haze of time, I well remember the name of the willing bride-to-be. She was Lily Bell Grimsby, the almost-sixteen-year-old daughter of the fanatical, narrow-minded speaker of the "Unknown Tongue." Far above the average in both intelligence and looks, she kept herself apart from the other students, perhaps because she knew that her father's strange behavior made her an object of mixed curiosity, ridicule, and pity. Disdaining the "nosiness" and crude jibes of her classmates and loathing their pity, she spent every free minute reading the books and magazines with which Paul, my town friends, and I now kept the school supplied.

Though she seemed oblivious of the boys and girls her age, my every wish was her command. Consequently, when I asked her to take the leading part in the play, she agreed, though I could see that the idea troubled her. Grieved by the lonely, tragic look, which habitually haunted her enormous violet eyes, I assigned the part to her, not because she had read it best, but because I wanted her to belong — to feel that she too had her place in the sun. I was actuated also by the knowledge that she could for a little while discard the drab, plain, dark dresses that she, as her father's daughter, was forced to wear. I planned to dress her in flaming red and bedeck her with flashy jewelry.

From the hour of the first rehearsal, however, I discovered that she was a natural; and the play, a foolish trivial skit, developed into what all of us knew would be a knockout. I reworded her lines, added a catchy song for her nice voice, and wrote in original scenes. In fact we practically

95

rewrote the play so that her talent could have greater latitude.

Determined to use every pupil in school (by this time about forty) I assigned speeches, worked up songs with pantomime and songs without action, trained folk dancers, and even created an original drill. For this I worked out the formations, special dance steps, and other action late one night to "Under the Double Eagle."

I went to bed wondering what I could use for three Mexican boys who had a keen sense of rhythm, and a poor command of the English language — too poor for me to make them objects of ridicule by assigning them speeches.

Though the school was beginning to accept the children of this nationality and include them in their play, I knew the parents had not developed such tolerance that they would accept the boys in the folk dances, particularly with the "white" girls. Besides, I salved my conscience, there was not room for that many in the dance.

Unable to sleep, I arose, slipped downstairs to the parlor, pulled down the shades, and turned on the light and the Victrola. The record on the machine was "Under the Double Eagle," hence, that was the music on which I built my "Clown Capers."

Fortunately, Mama and Papa were out at the farm, and Matt and my two sisters, Eugenia and Beulah, were sound sleepers; otherwise, they might have questioned my sanity as I counted and marched and shuffled and kicked, stopping only long enough to write down the figures that I liked, then beginning all over until the drill was complete, I thought. Cartwheels and somersaults were added later by the six versatile boys I chose to do the drill after they got into the spirit of the dance.

Why did I choose six boys? Well, that was the number of the first group to perform that particular drill, for the next afternoon, taking the Victrola and Genie, Beulah, and Matt, I went out to spend the weekend in Concrete, where

I planned to perfect the drill. When I found that these three were not enough to do the drill properly, I drafted Papa and my old country-school boyfriend, who had almost sidetracked my dream, and I joined in the dance myself. Mama, remaining true to her father's teaching, never in all her life indulged in any form of dancing, so she could not be included. The enlarged group proving to be just right for the drill, six was established as the number who would present it at the program.

11

As the date for the big event drew near, the whole community seethed with excitement. Many a weed in the cotton rows grew unmolested as those who should destroy it worked on or talked about the program.

Paul and his corps of schoolboy carpenters erected a temporary stage at one end of the building, set up temporary benches made of one-by-twelve boards on supports, and, using a large tarpaulin, constructed a dressing room outside and around the back entrance. They also gathered loads of moss, which I had assured them I must have.

From the best parts of worn-out cotton sacks, Mrs. Kimcek and Mrs. Wagner made a curtain for the stage, after dyeing the sacks a deep golden-yellow in a large iron washpot in which they had boiled the roots of some local shrubs to obtain the desired color. Mrs. Gholke, with the help of some of her neighbors, collected flour sacks, dyeing some of them red and bleaching the others to make them white. These sacks Mama used to make suits for our six clowns.

For our "Virginia Reel" and "Cotton-eyed Joe" I borrowed pioneer costumes from my Mohawk friends, who had recently used them for a masquerade ball. The little children who were singing and dancing "I See You" would

97

wear their Sunday best, as would those who were "saying speeches" or just singing.

As the loaded buggies, surreys, and wagons and the large groups on foot began to assemble about six o'clock for the barbecue that was to precede the program, Paul and I took one final survey of the waiting building, whose bare, drab walls had been completely cloaked with moss hung from ceiling to floor. Festoons of shining green smilax — "greenbrier vines," we called them — encircled the moss-covered walls, and the white blossoms of the hedge roses growing too abundantly, even then, along the fences in that area, added to the beauty of the moss and smilax. A few unlighted lanterns hung in the "main auditorium"; but behind the golden-yellow curtain, kerosene lamps with bright tin reflectors behind their carefully washed globes hung among the moss and smilax and wild roses, awaiting the match that would set them aglow for our big evening.

Wanting the transformation inside to be a surprise to the audience, we had earlier closed the blinds, not even permitting one glimpse to my family, who, most excited of all, had come out early to enjoy the festivities. Now, closing the door after one last satisfied look, Paul went out to check on the state of the meat on the large pit that had been dug down in the area which had once been Little Mexico. He was particularly interested in this part of the day's celebration, for he had furnished all the meat for the barbecue, while the women brought bread, cakes, pies, and potato salad made chiefly of mashed potatoes and big chunks of onion, over which vinegar was generously poured.

When we had closed the door, I went back to the tarpaulin-walled dressing room where Mama had drawn my bath — a bucket of cold water from the pump. With such essentials as towels and soap, she had brought the large mirror that usually hung over our marble-topped washstand at home, but which now hung on a large nail driven into the side of the schoolhouse wall.

Having finished my bath, I opened the large flat box, which I had the night before packed and left to be brought out in the family surrey. I had expected to find the carefully starched and ironed last summer's dimity dress I had packed to wear for the occasion. Instead, a soft yellow china silk dream-dress had replaced it. Its skirt was full, but it hugged my slender hips with rows of shirring; and rows of shirring outlined the slightly drop-shouldered neckline and finished the short sleeves. A wide, softly crushed, cream satin belt, much like today's popular cummerbund, gave it the finishing touch.

As an excited voice outside the tarpaulin shouted, "Teacher, come to supper!" I took one more glance in the mirror and went out "to knock their eyes out," as Paul later teasingly assured me.

At last the big moment for which we had worked so hard had arrived. The door was thrown open, and the awe-struck people packed the building from wall to wall. As I stood in front of the curtain, ready to greet the tense, expectant group, I felt humble and proud — and suddenly scared.

After a brief, sincere welcome and a rapid review of our harmonious year, I went out to the makeshift dressing room, where I found a state of complete confusion, for, like a terrible blight, over the hysterical group towered Mr. Grimsby, who had just exploded a devastating bombshell. In answer to their questions about Lily Bell's absence, he had snarled, "She is at home where you ort to be." And upon this cue, I entered.

Mr. Grimsby left me no time to wonder about the cause

of his visit, for as I stopped in the back door, he greeted me in his harsh, uncompromising voice. "If you're lookin' fer Lily Bell, she ain't here, and she ain't gonna be here. They's dancin' in this shindig and me and my family is agin dancin'. It's a tool of the devil."

In the midst of our pride and pomp, destruction had struck without warning!

Intrigued with my new dress, and reveling in the hesitant compliments and restrained praise of those who had only last fall looked at me with indifference or suspicion, I had not missed the Grimsby children. Now the show must go on — but how?

Signaling Pablo and Adolph to light the lamps and draw the curtain, I marched my first group of singers to the improvised stage, seated myself at the organ, and began the program. As I pumped the pedals of that organ and furiously pounded its keys, I thought desperately, "What shall I do?" I knew we could easily omit the speech that little Annie Grimsby so loved to say and the voice of Sam Grimsby, who "didn't want to do nothin' but sing," but without Lily Bell our program was ruined.

With my problem still unsolved, I struggled through my own particular medley of "Turkey in the Straw," and "Arkansaw Traveler" while the delighted boys and girls bowed and swung and sashayed through the "Virginia Reel."

Then as they got set for "Cotton-eyed Joe," a solution struck me — a solution that made me pound the keys harder to drown the pounding of my heart — I knew Lily Bell's lines! I could play her part!

Only my determination to thwart Mr. Grimsby, who had waited until the last minute for his denunciation of our program so that he could completely spoil it, made me finally decide to remove my yellow dress, put on the burnt-cork makeup and the flashy red costume Lily Bell was to wear; and take my place on the stage when the time came for "Axin' Papa's Permission."

Elated because they were to have their "hour upon the

100

stage," after their heartbreaking uncertainty, the others in the cast outdid themselves in this performance. Just one audible gasp from Mama and a sudden but immediately controlled start from Paul betrayed that anyone recognized the substitution for Lily Bell.

As the last number on the program, I had been persuaded, against my better judgment, to recite a poem of my students' choice. When at the end of the play I told them that we must omit that number, their disappointment seemed so great and they had been so wonderful that I was already wavering when Pablo, who was acting, with Adolph, as curtain puller and announcer, proclaimed proudly, "We will now listen to our nice teacher. She will say you 'Curfew Shall Not Ring Tonight'."

With difficulty, for my voice was choked with the tears I had held back so long, I began the highly sentimental poem, already worn out in the Gay Nineties. I tried to convert it to Negro dialect as I went along, adding gestures and strange postures to turn it into a comedy, in keeping with my makeup. Preoccupied with inventing dialect and gestures, my mind suddenly blacked out; and I stood for a lifetime, rooted to the floor. Finally, detemined not to "die on third base," I struck into a number from my old elocution days. Who its author was I do not know, for the copy I had clipped from the *Semi-Weekly News* and pasted lovingly in my scrapbook was marked "author unknown."

Its message, however, began with "Don't be what you ain't; jes be what you is," and ended with "It ain't what you is has been; it's what you now am is."

Maude Adams and Ethel Barrymore at the height of their glory never received more heartwarming tributes than were paid that night to a not-yet-eighteen-year-old girl who stood in an extremely short and exceedingly tight red dress, struggling without avail to halt the tears that flowed in a black stream down her dusky cheeks. The surrounding hills, it seemed, were echoing the applause of a simple, ap-

101

preciative people who would pay homage to this — their teacher.

12

Again that spring I was urged to take a place in town in the elementary school, a move that would eliminate the long horseback rides to and from Lost Creek and give me more prestige in the teaching profession, my friends argued. My interest, however, lay in teaching children in rural schools. They needed me, I felt.

Still a powerful force in my life too was my lodestar — "If a task is once begun, Never leave it till it's done" — and it, I think, really caused me to return to Lost Creek when fall came. I knew my task was not done.

Mr. Allan, a hard man but a man of his word, again signed the private contract for the bonus, as did Paul, though I would have gone back at the regular state pay.

When I left Lost Creek on Saturday afternoon, following another Cleanup Day to remove the no longer needed decorations and to prepare the building for Sunday School the next day, I was planning to attend school again that summer. Mama developed a serious illness late in May, however; and Papa, harassed by her illness and the interminable farm and store work, began to show evidences of the effects of his earlier long illness. Instead of going to school, therefore, I spent my summer helping take care of Mama, working in the store, and later in the summer weighing the cotton picked by Negro pickers hauled from town in wagons and housed in a little shack in the river bottom near the field.

Cotton, still as odious to me as it had always been, really proved a friend that summer, for illness requires money. Now the long rows of snowy cotton repaid my hatred with bales and bales of the fleecy staple, whose price increased as the tempo of war in Europe increased.

My summer was not all work, for Paul, almost every Sunday, drove his Model T Ford to bring me reports on Lost Creek activities, and Gus spent as many summer evenings in Concrete as he did in Cuero, though he had to hire a rig from the livery stable to make the long trip out to the country.

By the end of summer Mama was much improved, but Papa continued under the weather, as he expressed it. Therefore, when he received an offer for our store and farm, he sold both, and the family in the early spring moved to Humble, Texas, leaving Chico and me to finish the year boarding with a friend of mine in town.

My second year in Lost Creek followed closely the pattern of the previous year. There was the usual week at the County Institute where I was listed on the official printed program: "Discipline in Rural Schools, by Miss Cleo Winslett." And then later I rode with keen anticipation one morning late in September back to the community I had grown to love.

Paul insisted, on one of his visits to discuss school business, that he and the boys take care of Cleanup Day that year. Since he seemed particularly anxious to take care of it himself, I did not argue with him.

When I topped the hill and looked down on the spot where the old schoolhouse should be, I thought I was seeing a mirage, for on the spot where last year I had found a monstrosity of squalor and neglect, now stood a shining white schoolhouse with a dark-red roof. Surrounding this wonder was a neat, clean school yard, where the baseball diamond still occupied the most desirable spot. A well-drained area near the gate, however, had been leveled, and on it was a basketball court, on which a group of boys,

103

supervised by Paul, played with a new basketball.

Surrounded by a group of the patrons, who had again escaped the demands of King Cotton for a few hours and had come to see how Teacher liked her school, I walked into a transformed building, whose inside walls and ceiling were a soft cream color — "like the belt on your yellow dress" Paul told me later. In front of the now permanent stage hung a crude message done with red crayola on a flour-sack banner:

"Welcome Home, Teacher!"

On that day I had "intimations of immortality."

Though I had some disappointments and real griefs, my second year at Lost Creek was, I believe, more effective than the first. And as the year was nearing the end, with its busy, excited preparation for its barbecue and closing program, I knew that my mission at Lost Creek had been accomplished.

Two incidents during the year had brought sadness to me. None of the Grimsby children entered school that fall. When most of the cotton was gathered and still they did not come, I rode over to try to see Lily Bell and to persuade her father to send them back to school.

Lily Bell refused to come out, however, and Mrs. Grimsby stood embarrassed in the yard and told me they were too busy to have company. As I was about to turn Chico and leave, Mr. Grimsby, with a hangdog, evasive look, came up from the barn to tell me that the family was moving away in a few days; so the children would just wait to begin school in the new community. Though I asked where they were going, he did not answer. Baffled by Lily Bell's refusal to see me and her father's strange behavior, I rode away.

I learned later from a lawyer Mr. Grimsby had consulted that, in June following her father's destruction of

104

Lily Bell's happiness on the night she was to be in the play, an itinerant evangelist had stayed in the Grimsby home while he conducted a nearby protracted meeting, which developed into an emotional orgy. Mr. Grimsby had been elated when Brother Thomas devoted long hours "in prayer and Bible study" with the lonely, despondent Lily Bell, taking her for long walks after the services so he could "rassle with the devil," who had tempted her with such evils as "dancin' and playactin'. "

The meeting had finally come to an end and Brother Thomas had departed, assuring the proud family and their subdued daughter that he would soon be back, for he wanted to keep an eye on her so she would not be tempted to "stray from the fold." He had not returned and though Mr. Grimsby tried to trace him, he could not be found to furnish respectability, through marriage, to the desperate little pregnant girl.

The other event that brought me sadness came when I had to refuse Paul's request, made on Christmas Eve, after our Christmas program that I spend the rest of my life in his big white house on the hill overlooking Lost Creek School. His friendship was one of the finest experiences in my life and I did love him deeply, but the answer was no.

I sometimes wonder if the vision of King Cotton, stretching row after row between Lost Creek School and the inviting home of Paul Lawrence, was not the insurmountable barrier that influenced my answer.

As spring advanced and the end of school neared, Gus's visits grew more frequent and interesting. Consequently, while the crowd, packed into every available space to see the closing school program, stood and again cheered until the hills rang, I was once more overcome with tears, for I knew what none of them suspected — this was my final appearance on Lost Creek's stage. I was not only bidding good-bye to my beloved people but I was also bidding good-bye, I then thought, to the Dream that had so absorbed my life.

Though none of those present knew it, except Gus, who waited for me near the door, the next day I was to begin a new Dream — a Dream to last a lifetime — for I had finally agreed to marry the Mohawk Club member who, four years earlier, sat out a dance with me while he sang "Let Me Call You Sweetheart."

PART FOUR

Do It Well or Not at All

1

All the idealism, enthusiasm, energy, and love devoted to my early dream — that of being a good teacher — I now devoted to my new dream — that of being a good wife, and building, with the help of my young husband, a happy home. Always having been too busy teaching or being taught to spend any time on sewing, I now learned the thrill that comes from hanging a "ruffly" curtain, the product of my own skill with a needle. I discovered how the soft glow from a polished surface could reflect a soft glow in my own heart.

I had learned the thrill of cooking the year I was seven, when, as payment for the privilege of leaving the cotton patch and going to school, I stood on a box so that I could work at the cook table to prepare supper for our large, hungry family. That interest in cooking became even more intense as I grew older.

When I was at home, no other member of the family ever considered preparing supper. It was my job, and I wanted no suggestions nor distracting help. I liked to experiment with new recipes and invent new dishes of my own. In classroom or kitchen I wanted to "work out my own salvation."

Now, with wonderful new kitchen equipment and beautiful new dishes, linens, and silver, cooking was such a delight that as long as summer lasted I did not miss school at all. I must confess, though, that cooking for just two, instead of for rarely less than six and usually for ten or more, was a baffling experience. We often found ourselves with rice enough to feed a large segment of China or soup enough to keep a breadline healthy for at least a week.

We had a neighbor in the early days of our marriage, who, discovering my propensity for cooking more than we could eat, developed the habit of accidentally dropping in almost every day about the time Gus came home for lunch. Since she was old and alone and since she also furnished a means for disposal of some of the excess food whose abundance I never seemed able to control, we always invited her to eat with us. Though she always assured us she had already eaten and could not eat another bite, she always accepted our invitation and managed very effectively to help solve the problem posed by my prodigality in the kitchen.

Her constant presence on weekdays was not too great a nuisance, for Gus had to go back to work soon after lunch anyway. But her every-Sunday visit, which she extended on and on into the afternoon, irked us no end.

One Sunday, thinking we would thwart her, we stayed at home from church and had an early lunch. We hurried through the meal and were rushing the dishwashing so that the absence of any preparation of food might send her home early. (I had insisted we could not hurt her by locking the door.) Then we heard the click of our gate and saw her rushing up our front walk. She had not even stopped at home to remove the hat and gloves she had worn to church.

Leaving the unfinished dishes, I grabbed Gus, not troubling to relieve him of his dishcloth, and before he could protest, pulled him into the low, dark closet under the stairs that led from the kitchen to the attic. Then I

110

softly but definitely closed the door, ignoring the fact that the latch which opened the door, as well as closed it, was on the outside. There we crouched giggling in the dark. Well, I was giggling — I am not too sure about Gus.

We heard our friendly neighbor enter and look all through the house. Evidently she decided that we soon would return, for she finished the unwashed dishes and then sat down to wait in the little rocker I kept in the kitchen so that I could read in comfort while I worked. There she sat and rocked, humming the hymns she had heard at church that morning, while just inside the closet beside which she rocked we were folded, "stewing in our own juice," and not daring even to whisper.

When it seemed that we would be forced to cry "King's-ex," we heard her rise, search the house again — even the bathroom — and finally take a reluctant and, we were sure, puzzled departure. We forced ourselves to wait some time after the front gate clicked so that she would not hear the noise we would be forced to make when, in order to get out of our prison, we shattered the closet door.

I am not too sure even yet that Gus was not troubled about my sanity that day. My family had failed to brief him on my reaction to the "phonygraph," and the "red vision" the day I thought I had religion. He was therefore often somewhat overwhelmed by my impetuosities. He wisely insisted that a better way to rid ourselves of our too frequent visitor was to lock the door, but failing to do that, we should have finished the dishwashing and then rushed off to an urgent, fictitious engagement. His plan was more sensible, but I still think mine was more fun.

After all these years I still marvel at the "ways of marriage with a man and a maid." The product of a stern, straitlaced, highly conventional German family in whom a sense of humor was almost completely lacking and to whom life was truly real and earnest, Gus admitted that he was first attracted to me because of what he called my "sparkling gaiety and intoxicating happiness." I was so filled with fun, frivolity, and foolishness that he decided I was just the wife he wanted. Then having married the madcap I was, he spent the early part of our marriage trying to reform me.

The result was that, before many years had passed, I developed a bit of restraint and seriousness to season my impulsiveness, and he developed a sense of humor and some "fun and frivolity" of his own to brighten his seriousness. Thus is a good marriage strengthened and made lasting.

The first summer of our marriage had not ended before I was called to Humble because of Papa's sudden, desperate illness. Only a few hours after my arrival, he was gone. I was inconsolable, utterly lost, for with his gay laughter, his tender understanding, and his encouragement, he had been the axis around which my life had revolved. I knew that something which could never be replaced had gone, but I did not know for months what influence his death would have on the remainder of my life.

When the first September after our marriage came with its County Institute and its school days, my family and friends waited anxiously to see if I could resist the call of the classroom. As the days went by and I showed no evidence of a desire to go back to school, even refusing to accept a job only four miles from home, they sat back and relaxed, feeling that I truly meant to keep my promise to quit teaching. What nobody knew was that it took all the will power I could muster to stay at home and keep my agreement. I was truly devoted to my husband — I had made a bargain — I would stick to it.

2

One September afternoon a few years after we were married, I was particularly troubled about the situation in Humble, where Mama, with no training in anything but housework and rearing children, was struggling to keep my two sisters and my brothers in school. I decided to concentrate on some new dish for supper as a temporary respite from the problem I could not solve. This was a custom of mine; the more perplexing the problem, the more intricate the dish.

Searching through the stack of clippings I planned someday to paste in a special foods scrapbook, and the cookbooks, mostly free, that I had collected, I came upon my old *How to Teach School,* as I had done for years before when I was temporarily sidetracked by a baseball and the owner of a red bicycle. Just to look at my treasure engulfed me in a wave of homesickness for school. Forgetting what I had planned to do, I sat reading its pages and reliving my Dream, until the demanding call of my little son, who was awake after his nap, brought me back to reality.

But that afternoon as Floyd (my little son) and I went for the walk we both enjoyed so much, I found it difficult to thrill over all the lovely things he found to share with me — a dusty little flower struggling up by the concrete walk, a friendly spotted puppy that tried to give him a kiss, an empty little snail house lying forgotten under a weed, a bright-colored rock that he could hold tight in his tiny hand and take home to show Daddy. My preoccupa-

113

tion, I suspect, was his first intimation that he had a rival — never in my heart, however, but just in my interests.

"If I could go back to teaching," kept tantalizing me, "I could relieve the situation in Humble. And something must be done, but what? If I could — " Again my thoughts would complete their circle and start over.

Serving meals to hungry oil field workers who flocked eagerly to enjoy the bountiful food she served in her little home, Mama had been able to keep the children fed, clothed, and in school. But the effort had taken its toll of her strength and health, and now it was evident that she could not continue such hard work. Gus and I knew that we must come to her aid. To take her out of the kitchen, therefore, we hired a Mexican nurse, a jewel indeed, to take care of our adored son — and I again took up teaching school.

As long as she lived, Mama grieved over what she thought was my great sacrifice for her. She never could believe, though I tried to convince her, that what she really did was furnish me with the excuse I needed to go back to the work I loved and to follow again the Dream I had never relinquished.

3

We were living in Laredo when we finally decided I should go back to teaching. Things were booming, and the schools were bursting at their seams. As a result of this crowded condition, I was offered a very unusual job, even before I had solicited it. I was given thirty problem children, whom I was to try to control and teach in an adobe building across the street from Central School. I was told that they would not study and would not behave, and I was urged to handle them any way I thought best.

The classroom was a two-room apartment with hard-packed dirt floors. Its back door opened on a bare, dusty

114

quadrangle, which was called a patio by the poor families who, with their numerous children, chickens, and goats, were our neighbors. Often the busy chickens or an inquisitive goat would stroll into our classroom. And the curious but shy neighbors would peep around the door, or, placing a chair or a stool just outside in their "patio," they would sit and watch us at our work.

Several of the young misfits who were assigned to me were from prominent families. Some of them had been expelled from several schools, though they were only in the fourth grade. Consuelo Jordan, a bitter twelve-year-old girl, was brought across the river from Nuevo Laredo, Mexico, each morning in a large limousine driven by a liveried chauffeur. She was the daughter of an American man who had married her Mexican mother, then deserted her when his family in the States would not accept her. Later the mother had married a Japanese art collector. Consuelo was unhappy in school in Mexico, and she hated school in America. She did not seem to belong anywhere.

Relying on my already tested precepts, I kept my young misfits busy, treated them all with real respect, played with them, believed in them, and soon loved them very dearly. Though the teachers were not required to do any sort of supervision outside the classroom, I organized a baseball club that soon took on all challengers. We even became so enthusiastic about baseball that we took a half day off from school one day and went out to see two Big League teams play an exhibition game.

When I broached my plan to Mr. Christian, the superintendent — a kind, lovable, understanding old fellow who, with only a specially-issued city certificate, had headed Laredo's schools for almost a half century — he said, "Whatever you do with those kids to change them is all right with me. Do what you wish, but you don't have to make up the half day."

We did make up the half day, however, for I did not want the other teachers in the system to feel that my class

115

enjoyed special privileges (an unfortunate tendency among teachers). In those days many hard-working, successful teachers were called the "boss's bootlicker," later the superintendent's "fair-haired lady," and more recently a "D. E. B." (Damned Eager Beaver).

I insisted that we would make up the day, too, because I wanted to test the loyalty and appreciation of the group and because I wanted them to know they could not have something for nothing. Consequently, the Saturday morning we would make up the half day was set, and at nine o'clock that morning all thirty pupils were in that little adobe building.

They were truly the most brilliant group I have ever had in one class. Bored by the simple work necessary for non-English-speaking members of their classes, they had occupied their class time thinking up new ways to annoy their teacher. The teachers, instead of giving them something to keep them busy, had tried force to control them. One teacher did practice a novel method for control. She kept a giant-sized bottle of castor oil, which she dished out in generous doses to those she would discipline. One boy told me seriously that he would rather take the castor oil than the class. Here again I had found Lost Creek assembled all in one grade.

The prescribed course of study set up by a supervisor, who had been recruited that year from the State Department in an attempt to establish citywide coordination and standards of achievement for Laredo's elementary schools, furnished a fresh challenge to the members of my class, who were too intelligent to be unaware of the reason their teachers had gladly sent them over to the adobe hut to me. Added to their desire to outshine their more favored contemporaries was their innate ability, plus the prodding of my competitive spirit, which was kept at white heat always by my lodestar poem with its closing challenge: "Do it well or not at all."

All these factors entered into the result of the first
116

school-wide achievement tests based on our new course of study and administered and graded by our supervisor. The entire city was amazed at the grades made by my "incorrigibles," for our record of achievement made the front page in the local paper, which, incidentally, was owned by the father of my heretofore worst problem child. "Fine Buildings Do Not Make Fine Schools," he had begun his article.

When that fall we were offered a nice room in the regular building, my pupils and I chose to remain in our own little republic, whose dirt walls had been transformed with bright rugs, serapes, colorful strings of peppers, gourds and other dried plants, pictures made of feathers, and picturesque pottery from many parts of Mexico — all contributions from my incorrigibles.

The unused room of the two-room apartment, the first year, had stood like a gaping, musty cavern, to whose walls the odor of bats and goats and unwashed people still clung. In its dark, dusty recesses enormous sand fleas multiplied, and waxed fat in the fertile feeding grounds in the adjacent room. Lazy lizards draped themselves to sun on the sill of the one high, small window. And one day during class we saw a rattlesnake slither from its dark recesses and halt in the doorway that entered our room.

But now the empty cavern had become a thing of beauty and a joy to my pupils — a room where a pupil with time to spare could sit and read or just dream. The admission fee to this room was work, ready and well done.

The insects and reptiles were banished, along with the dark, by our appreciative newspaperman, who had the insects exterminated and the dark and heat banished with good lights and a large fan. He also furnished two large, comfortable chairs and a small settee.

Gus, who had assumed a lifelong responsibility when he volunteered to make the doll cradle for my Lost Creek children, built shelves from floor to ceiling along one wall and made two strong study tables. All these he painted a

117

soft green. With these furnishings, with colorful serapes to cloak the ugly walls, with magazines and newspapers to invite the imagination, the room was a haven of quiet and peace and joy — something most of these boys and girls had never known.

We were still in our private republic for the third year and had become seventh graders, known all over Laredo as the Trusty Thirty. But during the Christmas holidays, disaster (or so it seemed to me at that time) overtook us. My husband was leaving Laredo to become manager of a lumberyard in Edna on the first of the new year; hence, I must leave my little republic and go to our new home as soon as the Laredo School Board would release me.

I therefore stood one night in early March by the impatiently chugging train that would take me out of the lives of a group of children I had come to love very much. Surrounding me stood my Trusty Thirty, who had come to the depot at eleven o'clock at night to shower me with gifts — and tears. Finally the train gave a particularly insistent, plaintive whistle; and, almost blinded by my tears, I climbed the steps on the car, carrying my sleepy son, whom I had been forced to drag from his wailing nurse, Francisca.

I was a long time in Edna before I could hear the plaintive whistle of a train on a still night and not feel that it was the call of my Trusty Thirty.

4

Reports of my work in Laredo preceded me to Edna, for my thoughtful, appreciative superintendent, who was soon to yield to the demands of modern education and transfer his life's work to a successor with a college degree, had written the Edna School Board about me. Two days after I landed in Edna I received, as the result of his letter, a telephone call from the president of the school board, telling me that I had been elected to teach in Edna's school system the next year. I had not applied and he did not know me. He had read the letter to the assembled school board (a new superintendent was hired that night too) and they had elected me "sight unseen."

Though Gus had felt that with his new status and increased pay we could keep up both our home and Mama's without my teaching, the pull of my Dream was too strong. When the unsolicited, unexpected offer came, I signed a contract to teach in Edna's Public Schools, a contract that continued for much more than a quarter of a century — the happiest and most satisfying years of my life.

Through the close, muggy, intolerably hot summer I longed for the comforts I had enjoyed in Laredo. I loathed every inch of the little country town whose water was furnished by windmills in every yard, whose lights went off at midnight, whose problems of sewage and garbage disposal belonged to each family, and whose streets were hog wallows when the rains came and dusty trails when the rains ceased.

Vividly impressed on my memory is the picture of a sign on Main Street in the very heart of the two-block business section after a long rainy period. It read: "Detour. This Is Hell!"

I did not completely believe the message until one day we, having ignored the warning, discovered that it was too, too true. Passing the sign, we rode into the sea of mud in our Model T. Finding that we could go neither forward nor backward, I got out to push, since I had not yet learned to drive our new Ford. I had also not yet learned the consequences of standing immediately behind the rear wheel of an automobile stuck in black mud. My fury, when I learned, furnished the power to help us out of the

119

mudhole, I am sure, for it could almost have moved mountains.

Before I seated myself on the papers Gus had carefully spread to protect the upholstery from the mud that enveloped me, I wiped some more mud out of my eyes, located the carpenter's heavy-leaded pencil on the floor of our car, and waded through the sticky mud to the sign, in spite of my scandalized husband's protest. There I added in bold strokes: "This Is a Gross Understatement!"

That summer I gave more thought to the problems I would face in school in Edna than I had given even to those at Lost Creek, for now the careers of two people and the future of a third were involved. If I should make serious mistakes or fail, it would not only affect my life and lives of those I taught, but it would also affect the lives of my husband and my son. I therefore faced a greater responsibility, I felt, than ever I had faced before.

First, I knew that I must learn to work with other teachers and to consider their desires as well as my own. In Rosebud and Lost Creek I had made my own plans and decisions and had accepted the consequences of my acts. In Laredo I was attached to Central School, insofar as being listed on its staff and being included in its annual report were concerned, but I was still very much a lone wolf. I was responsible in reality, only to the superintendent, who had turned the job over to me, much as Mr. Coffin had left me the job at Lost Creek. He had asked for results but had not attempted to dictate how those results should be achieved.

In Edna, however, I knew I must work in a building with other teachers, all of whom had been in their positions for years and so ranked above me in priority and prestige. I must defer to a principal whose wishes I must consult before I attempted any unorthodox movements or reforms. I must school myself to conform to a pattern — an attainment I have not yet fully achieved, for, like my grown-up, tight shoes and my hobble skirt on the memor-

120

able buggy ride, a cut-and-dried pattern still "cramps my style."

Added to this problem of adjusting to work with a group, was a much more dangerous and vexing problem that had bedeviled Gus and me all that summer. We soon discovered that we had come into a community that was riddled by bitternesses and intolerances left by the backwash of the Ku Klux Klan. Sisters met sisters face to face and did not see each other. Neighbors whose yards joined had not spoken to each other in years. "Ku Klux Klan children" disliked playing with "anti-Klan children," and naturally all this strife had found its way into the schools.

Shortly after I arrived in Edna we received an invitation to attend a meeting of the slowly dying Klan. This invitation we declined graciously but firmly. Shortly thereafter we were amazed to learn that I was a Catholic and Gus a Jew. I suppose my reply, made in answer to a question about my nationality, that I was chiefly Irish furnished the basis for my classification, and the *witz* ending of our name was responsible for Gus's being called a Jew. The real reason, we both know, lay in our lack of interest in the Klan.

Knowing all these problems I must meet, however, did not tempt me to abandon my desire to continue teaching. I thought of old Mr. Parker with his chewing tobacco and his narrow, dogmatic opinions. I thought of the outlaw Jenkins boys, who had apparently developed into good citizens. I thought of my Lost Creek School, which had changed from an eyesore and a source of trouble to a place where the whole community could come for knowledge and inspiration. I thought of my Trusty Thirty, who had amazed a whole city with their regeneration. And I knew that He who had guided my "certain flight" thus far would again "lead my steps aright."

I arose early on the morning my new job was to begin, helped my excited little son get ready for his first day of

121

school, and then "put on my armor" for the task that lay ahead.

Wanting to make a good first impression, I brushed my newly bobbed hair and carefully dressed myself in a gold-colored dress whose belt girdled my hips and whose skirt hem just tipped my knees. Then, filled with mingled trepidation, anticipation, and excitement, I walked down the street to my new job, while the large bell in its church-like steeple on top of the schoolhouse rang a loud, slow-measured "Ding! Dong!" to remind pupils and teachers that a new school year was beginning.

One of my disillusioned teacher-friends, who, after a lifetime of successful and devoted service, was being discarded like a once-plump orange sucked dry, parodied Byron in her bitterness: "Whom the gods hate, they make schoolteachers." And she had reason to feel exactly as she did.

In spite of all the trials, heartaches, and reverses that I have met in teaching boys and girls, however, my parody would be: "Whom the gods love, but would test, they make schoolteachers."

If
Some mystic necromancer,
Rising from the dusty sands of the long lane
Down which I walked toward Rosebud School
One bright September morning long ago,
Had, like the apparition in *Macbeth,* held up his
    magic mirror,
Revealing all the years that intervened from then
    till now,
Then asked, "What dream do you choose,
    young one?"
I might have paused
    And thought
        And even shuddered
At some tragic episode the glass foreshadowed;

Yet
Knowing all,
My answer would have come strong and
    unfaltering:
"I'll buy that dream, Sir. Bring the Challenge on!"